Teaching Writing:
A Workshop Approach

By
Adele Fiderer

S C H O L A S T I C
PROFESSIONAL BOOKS

NEW YORK • TORONTO • LONDON • AUCKLAND • SYDNEY

ACKNOWLEDGMENTS

This book had its beginnings with the Scarsdale Teachers Institute course *Writing for Publication* given in the fall of 1991. I was the teacher/coordinator of the course, and Terry Cooper of Scholastic, Inc., assisted throughout in its planning and execution. The course was strengthened by the appearance of several of Scholastic's editors who helped me and my colleagues believe that we had something of value to write and—what was even more incredible to us—that we actually could write.

I am especially grateful to Joyce Senn, my editor at Scholastic, whose enthusiasm and written suggestions were invaluable in helping me see where I had to think harder and write better.

Teachers who have commented on the manuscript-in-progress include my daughter, Beebe Allyson Garcia, and I thank her. I am also grateful to Valerie Rein, Margaret O'Farrell, Janet Perkins, and Jean Little whose students' work appears in this book.

To my own students, past and present, I owe my gratitude for examples of their work and for the countless ways they helped me learn more about teaching writing.

Finally, a special thanks to Martin for believing I could finish this book.

Design by Jacqueline Swensen
Cover Design by Vincent Ceci
Cover Art by Bari Weissman
Interior Illustration by Maxie Chambliss
Edited by J.A. Senn

ISBN 0590-49202-0

Copyright © 1993 by Adele Fiderer

12 11   23/0

Printed in the U.S.A.

Table of Contents

Introduction

In 1981, assisted by writing researcher Lucy McCormick Calkins, teachers in my district began to experiment with a workshop, or process, approach to teaching writing. Since that time, we have seen remarkable changes in our students as writers and in ourselves as writing teachers. Most exciting of all was the change in the way our students felt about writing. Pleading at the end of a writing workshop, "Do we have to stop writing?", our children now show us how much they love to write.

Of course, change wasn't easy. As we developed a new set of beliefs about how children learn to write, we found ourselves struggling with both challenging and practical issues. For example, because we felt authentic learning experiences were important, we gave up worksheets and single paragraph assignments and encouraged students to write whole and personally meaningful texts. We also came to realize that good writing takes time. Writing involves thinking and rethinking, revising and rewriting and plenty of opportunities throughout the process to talk about ideas. As a result, we changed our curriculum and daily schedules by abandoning once-a-week writing periods in favor of four or five workshops a week.

Responding to our students' writing proved to be another challenge. Instead of red-penning corrections and comments on their papers after they had finished writing, we had to learn how to talk with and listen to our students *while* they were writing. Of course, because we were terribly concerned about what the rest of the children would be doing while we were conferring with some, we learned new ways to organize materials and space in our classrooms, and we developed predictable routines for the students to follow.

Over the years we encountered additional problems and situations that led to more learning. Full of questions, even doubts, we struggled to find solutions in our own classrooms. Many issues arose—for example, what place direct instruction had in a writing workshop and how our students would learn grammar and the conventions of writing if they did not use workbooks. We also wondered how the workshop approach would help students improve their writing in other curriculum areas, and of course, evaluation was another big concern. What procedures could we develop to make writing assessment meaningful and manageable?

What helped us most as we experimented with these issues was our willingness to take risks and to support each other as we reflected on our problems and discoveries. It is these discoveries—specific strategies, procedures, and materials that worked best for us and our students—that I will share with you in this book.

During the past 12 years, I have worked each morning in a suburban school district as a consulting teacher in the classrooms of my colleagues and in the afternoons as a classroom teacher of writing and reading. I have also served as a consultant to teachers in an urban school district with many more problems than ours. The suggestions and examples of student work that appear in this book are drawn from my own experiences in these many different classrooms from second through sixth grade. I hope they will help you deal with situations and issues that relate to your teaching of writing. You should also feel free to use them in your own way to create a writing workshop based on your students' needs and the unique expertise and interests that you bring to your teaching.

CHAPTER ONE

Organizing a Writing Workshop

Anyone who teaches knows that moving from a traditional approach to a process-oriented, hands-on curriculum involves fundamental changes. Such a move means much more than simply adopting new activities and strategies. It means giving students choices, responsibilities, and the opportunity to interact while they write. For me, it also meant giving up a large measure of control in order to guide my students toward independence.

These changes weren't easy at first; they made me find new ways to organize my time, materials, and the classroom setting itself, and meanwhile I had to keep everything running smoothly. Ultimately, however, it was worth the struggle because my formerly silent, once-a-week writing period in which students completed my assignments with little enthusiasm was transformed into a daily, active workshop in which students loved to write. This chapter describes my workshop approach to teaching writing while offering you some basic guidelines for organizing workshops in your classroom. At the end of the chapter, illustrated vignettes will also take you on a guided tour of a typical workshop.

THE MEANING OF A WORKSHOP

Workshop—a setting in which artists or craftsmen are involved in a variety of hands-on creative activities. A workshop leader is a facilitator, working with individuals or small groups and doing very little up-front lecturing.

By thinking of your classroom as a workshop where writers, like artists, craft their individual works over time, you are more likely to create the kind of individualized and interactive learning environment that best supports the writing process. For example, in a workshop, activities will vary because writers tend to work on individual projects at their own pace. A few students might be planning or researching a new writing topic while others may be writing rough drafts, and still some other writers might be revising while others are correcting and recopying a completed draft.

A workshop is interactive as well as individualized. The feedback writers receive gives them the impetus to keep going and to improve their writing. That means you can expect to hear the soft buzz of writers reading and talking about their work as you listen to individual students and ask relevant questions.

THE ORGANIZATION OF A WORKSHOP

Many teachers ask me how an individualized and interactive workshop approach can be orderly and manageable. Part of the answer

to this question lies in the organization and accessibility of writing materials. I set up my classroom at the beginning of the year with a wide choice of writing tools and materials in a particular area, and then I invite my students, for example, to help themselves to paper when they need it. I always keep a variety of different sizes and colors of paper, lined and unlined, on the shelves of a large, deep bookcase.

Also on the shelves are tools for writing—such as a date stamp, scissors, scotch tape, staplers, and staple removers. I also provide several dictionaries, thesauruses, and laminated samples of friendly and business letters. Publishing tools, which I also make available, include a hole-punch, yarn, peel-off vinyl letters and plastic letter stencils for creating book titles, cloth tape for book spines, as well as cardboard and oaktag sheets and adhesive shelf paper for making book covers. Of course, I take some time to introduce these materials to my students and discuss their uses and care early in the year.

In another accessible area I place a collection of picture books, poetry, plays, magazines, short story anthologies, travel brochures, and non-fiction books. These books and materials serve as sources and models to help students learn about writers' techniques and the wide variety of forms that written products can take.

A rack holding the students' cumulative writing folders sits on top of the bookcase. Cumulative folders, or portfolios, contain writing pieces along with the drafts that students complete throughout the year. Periodically my students and I review these portfolios to assess their progress.

A third area is for editing materials. Plastic trays hold peer-editing and spelling practice forms. A box labeled "Editor-in-Chief" contains student-edited drafts for me to check. (*Descriptions of these and other editing materials are in Chapter 4, pages 43–59.*)

On the classroom walls are reference charts that my students and I developed to help them work independently. Chart titles include the following. (*For examples of these and other charts, see pages 98–103 in the Appendix.*)

- How to Find a Topic.
- What Writers Do.
- What to Do When You Are Stuck.
- How to Help a Writer.
- Marks for Revising and Editing.
- Am I Ready to Edit?

I also create areas where students can easily display their published work in the corridor outside the classroom and in the room itself. Because I have limited space, I string two wires across the room for writing displays. We are also fortunate to have a computer in our classroom and a computer lab in our school. These computers and our school's photocopy machine enable us to publish multiple copies of newsletters and grade level anthologies of students' writing.

Each student's desk contains individual writing materials. There is a sturdy folder with pockets to hold writing-in-progress drafts and editing guideline forms, a writing notebook or journal, pencils, and crayons or markers. Upper elementary students also normally use pens and liquid paper correction fluid.

THE RITUALS AND ROUTINES THAT SUPPORT A WORKSHOP

By organizing materials in advance and making them available to students, I have taken some steps toward establishing an orderly and manageable workshop. In order to achieve this goal, however, I also develop rituals and routines so that students will know what they will be expected to do at particular times. For example, I begin the year by setting aside consistent and frequent blocks of time for writing. Because I let my students know the days and times they will be writing, they realize that they are expected to write when workshop time arrives. Planning ahead also has another advantage. When students know they will write on a particular day, many will make plans for their writing in advance.

I also decide which areas will be used for writing conferences and peer sharing. A group conference with me, for example, always takes place at a round table with several chairs. Peer conferences are held on the periphery of the room in pre-determined areas—either on the rug or on chairs. During sharing time, a special stool or author's chair is reserved for the writer while the rest of us gather around—some on chairs and others on a rug. There is also a routine for signing up to share. Students who want feedback from the class on their writing that day simply write their names below the word *Sharing* on the blackboard.

Then I plan how the workshop time will be used. Since I believe that students should spend most of the hour writing and conferring, I allot only a few minutes for teaching a mini-lesson and another brief period for students to share their writing with the class. Some years I introduce each writing workshop with a mini-lesson and conclude it with a sharing time. Other years I teach a mini-lesson before sharing time because it seems to work better to have students move into writing after a period of silent reading. You see, there really is no one way to organize the components of a writing workshop—as long as there are predictable rituals and routines that allow children to take responsibility for much of their own learning.

THE LOOK AND SOUND OF A WRITING WORKSHOP

If you are like me and most teachers I know, you gain new insights about teaching by visiting other classrooms to observe teachers and students at work. This section will attempt to do the next best thing through illustrated vignettes. You will "see" many of the activities and materials that you would observe in a visit to one of my writing

quick survey to determine my students' plans for writing that day. The survey tells me something about each student's progress and lets me know who may need a writing conference that day. The survey also helps my students focus in on what they will be doing that day.

SURVEY OF DAILY WRITING PLANS		
	5/25	5/27
Liz B.	Editing conf.	Write good copy
Greg G.	Notebook	Draft "Wayside"
Daren	Topic conf.	Draft "Cindy Yella"
Stefano	Storyboard	Storyboard conf.

Every day students spend about 30 to 35 minutes engaged in a variety of writing activities. Reference charts help them work independently and free me to confer with individuals or small groups.

Group conferences are held at a round table. I model the role of conferencer so that my students will learn how to conduct a writing conference. In another classroom area, Amanda and Liz are discussing ideas for new writing topics.

A draft conference often leads to revision.

workshops. These activities and materials will, then, be described in greater detail in the remaining chapters.

To begin this workshop, I gather students together for a mini-lesson. In the lesson I show them how the use of specific words—instead of general words—makes writing more interesting.

Two or three times each week, I take a

AM I READY TO EDIT?

Name:_____

Name of Editing Partner?_____

Title: _____

1. I read the writing to myself to see if it made sense.   _____

2. I read it to my partner to see if it made sense.   _____

3. My writing is focused on one important topic.   _____

4. I developed the topic with enough information.   _____

TRY AGAIN!

Name _____ Date _____

Word	FirstTry	Second Try	Standard Spelling

READER'S COMMENTS

Title: Tornado!
Author: Jane Kim

READER	COMMENTS
James R.	I liked the part when the tornado almost blew you away.
Karen	Your pictures are great.
Mrs. Wolf	Your lead really grabbed me!

Students revise in many different ways; for example, some prefer to cut and paste, but others pencil in arrows to show where one part is to be moved. A few others want to rewrite the draft. I also discuss revision strategies with my students in mini-lessons and during our daily sharing time.

Not all students are in the process of developing a writing piece that will be published. For example, Felipe and Cheryl are writing in their notebooks. Later they will use some of the ideas in these exploratory notebook entries as topics for writing projects.

The editing area is equipped with checklists as well as handbooks on the conventions of writing. A reference chart guides students through the editing process, which can involve self-editing, peer-editing, and teacher editing. Writing folders also contain individual editing checklists such as the one shown on page 11.

During an editing conference with Chris, I copy his misspelled words on this "Try Again" form and show him how to correct his run-on sentences.

A few students are ready to publish today. They will place their handmade books in the classroom library for students in other classrooms to read. Student writing is also displayed on bulletin boards in hallways and hung from wires stretched across the classroom. Young authors always enjoy comments made by other students, parents, and teachers.

Robbie has removed his writing from the

I think that my best writing so far is the letter I wrote to President Bush. I used specific words to describe the dirty streets in the city and the homeless people and asked him to help. He wrote back and thanked me for writing.

Draft
32 Clark Road
South Hills, NY 11145-
November 17, 1995

President Bush
The White House
Washington DC 11144. (?)
Dear President Bush
I am writing this letter to ask

bulletin board today and is placing it in his cumulative writing folder. I discuss the collected pieces with parents at conference time and point out evidence of growth. Periodically students review and assess their own writing.

My students look forward to their ten-minute sharing time at the end of a writing workshop. Today, for example, Scott is eager to get his classmates' responses to his story about his father's early school days. "Should I put in the part at the end about hearing kids running and stamping down the stairs?" he asks.

Sharing
Scott
Sally
Jillian

Questions Teachers Ask About Organizing and Managing a Workshop

Q I have 34 students in my second grade classroom: when they all write at the same time, it gets noisy. I see students talking, and I'm not sure whether they are working productively. What can I do?

A Often students just need brief assistance to keep going, but sometimes having a very large number of students makes this difficult. Following are several strategies that have worked for me and other teachers.

1. Let some students go off by themselves to curl up in corners and write on clipboards or lap trays. Then rearrange the seating to give other students more space.

2. Move about the room to confer individually with students instead of sitting at a table with a group. Let your students know your "route" and suggest strategies they can use if they don't know how to proceed while waiting for you. (See page 100,) "What to Do When You Are Stuck."

3. Train parent and grandparent volunteers to assist for at least two hours a week. Volunteers need to understand the writing process approach and the routines and materials that support a workshop. After being trained by the teacher for an hour or so and observing her activities during a writing workshop, the parents are able to help.

4. Divide the class into two groups. Students in both groups participate in the workshop's mini-lesson and sharing time in the morning. Then Group A writes for about half an hour while Group B reads silently off to one side of the classroom. In the afternoon Group B writes while Group A reads silently.

5. In some schools a reading teacher comes to the classroom during writing workshop time to confer with students who are scheduled to receive skills help. Working as a team, the classroom and reading teacher help more students than one teacher working alone. You might want to explore a similar collaboration with your school's reading specialist.

Q I have to teach science, math, health, literature, and social studies. How can I find time for hour-long writing workshops four or five times a week?

A Following are some ways you might be able to manage to find sufficient time for writing.

1. Integrate writing into the various disciplines. Your students can develop writing projects during their workshop time that pull together the learning experiences they had in a particular subject area. All writing pieces, whether the topic is based on a personal or content area experience, are developed through the process of drafting, conferring, and revising.

2. Have an hour-long writing workshop two days each week. Shorten writing times on one or two additional days to 30 minutes by omitting mini-lessons and sharing time.

3. "Chunk" writing workshops into three week segments. One segment of daily workshop writing is followed by a three week period in which your students focus on other curriculum areas. During these periods have your students write in their writing notebooks for ten to fifteen minutes a day.

CHAPTER TWO

Setting the Stage for Writing

Anyone who has ever tried to record personal thoughts on paper for others to read knows the sense of risk that writing involves. To write honestly about what they know, all writers, especially youngsters, need to know that they have something of value to say. They also need to know that their ideas will be received with respect by a supportive community. Therefore, in the first weeks of the school year, my students create projects and crafts that invite them to share personal interests and experiences. After these activities, they are ready for writing notebooks, in which they will write about memories, experiences, opinions, words, and ideas. The content of these notebooks will produce many seeds for writing topics throughout the school year.

PERSONAL SHARING

On the first day of school in September, I let my students know that they will be doing several enjoyable projects so that we can get to know each other. Because the projects provide lots of ideas for notebook writing, they will create individual "All About Me" folders to collect the forms, interviews, drawings, and writings produced at this time. Then I circle the date of our first writing workshop on a large calendar. Brimming with ideas for their first topic, my students are always ready and eager to write when that day arrives.

ACTIVITIES FOR SHARING

Personal sharing, which teachers use to encourage self-discovery, can be accomplished through a wide variety of games, projects, and crafts—some of which are discussed below. Not only will you enjoy doing one or two of the projects along with your students, but your participation will also enhance the feeling of community in your classroom. Since many sharing activities take place in small groups, your students should discuss guidelines for working in groups. In fact, you may want to use the following questions to help them brainstorm their own guidelines.

✦ How do you take turns?

✦ How do you listen to others?

✦ How do you respond to another person's ideas?

Photo Biographies

Have your students bring in old and recent photographs that have special meaning to them. If possible, enclose the photos in page protectors or photocopy them and return the originals for safekeeping. You can give each child a strip of sturdy paper to display the photos along with captions that tell something about each picture. For example, a fifth grade student brought in a photograph that showed her telling a story to her classmates. Her caption read, "I am telling the story 'The Ghost With One Black Eye.' I learned the story from my grandma. My grandma heard it from her old neighbors son. In this picture I am telling how the ghost got scared and jumped out the window."

Some teachers ask their students to bring in individual albums that display several photos with captions describing each important event. Since parents enjoy helping their children with such a project, you may want to ask them to include a letter reflecting on memories of their child.

Note Writing

Make "mailboxes" for you and each student out of shoe boxes or large cloth shoe bags with pockets. On the first day of school place a note in each mailbox that tells something about you, and then invite your students to write a note back to you or to a classmate telling about themselves. Let them know that they don't need to worry about correct spellings.

Time Lines.

Provide your students with several index cards and crayons or colored pens. Ask them to write or draw on each card one picture of something important that happened to them (moved, new baby sister, first bicycle). Your students should then arrange the cards in chronological order, and those who are able should write their age or the year of the event on each card. After they punch a hole in each of the four corners of each card, they should thread two lengths of yarn through the holes. When they are finished, they will have created a personal time line of their lives. Then have them meet in small groups to share their time lines. When the sharing is over, you may want to hook the time lines onto hangers for display.

Interest Inventories.

Distribute interest inventory forms. (*See Figure 1, which follows.*) If you teach young children, read aloud the sentence stems for them to complete with words or drawings. Encourage your students to add additional stems they can complete to reveal more about them and their interests (e.g., I belong to, I used to like, I like to visit). Let them know

FIGURE 1

INTEREST INVENTORY

1. There are _____ people in my family, counting me.

   They are _____

   _____

   _____

2. My favorite kind of pet is a _____

   _____

3. I am really good at _____

4. I collect _____

5. Something I really like to do is _____

6. Something I don't like doing is _____

7. The one thing that means the most to me is _____

   because _____

8. My special friend is _____

9. I take lessons in _____

10. Here is something else you should know about me _____

    _____

invented spellings are acceptable.

You also may want to assign each student a private number to identify his or her interest inventory instead of including names. The interest inventories can then be distributed, read aloud, or posted on a bulletin board so that other students can guess the name of the person who fits each description.

What's on Your Mind?

Provide all of your students with a "What's On Your Mind" form. (*See Figure 2, which follows.*) Ask them to write their responses to the questions in each box, or you may prefer to have them draw their own profiles of a head in which they can draw or write about people, things, or events in their lives. (*See Figure 3 on page 20.*) After showing your students your own profile, have them get together in small groups to share their drawings and writing.

Paper People.

Give your students pieces of mural paper that match their heights. Then have them work in pairs to trace the outlines of their bodies. After drawing and coloring in hair, clothing, and features, they should cut out the paper dolls. (Strips of cardboard or a ruler taped in back of the cutout's neck will keep the heads from flopping over.) When your students are ready to "introduce" their cutouts to classmates, they should describe the special interests they outlined on their interest inventory forms. To give their parents a delightful surprise on Open School Night, ask your students to "sit" the cutouts in their chairs. If you teach young children, you may want to invite upper grade students, or parents, to do the tracing, cutting, and interviewing for this activity.

Person to Person-Scavenger Hunt.

To prepare for this scavenger hunt, distribute one index card to all of your students. Then ask them to write a sentence on the card that tells about something they are good at or something special they own. (Be sure that they do not write their names on the cards.) After you collect the cards, write a follow up question on each one—such as "How did you

learn to do that?" or "What does it look like?" Then distribute the cards, making sure that no student receives his or her own. Without showing their card to anyone, your students should look for the person who fits the particular description on their card by asking questions. When they locate the individual who wrote the sentence, they should write that person's name on the card and ask the follow-up question and any others they can think of. Stop the activity after everyone has been identified. You also may want your students to gather together to name the person and share their information. This is a good recess activity because it requires all students to move about and talk for about ten or fifteen minutes. When the sharing is over, return the cards to their writers, who should then place them in their folders.

Partner Interviews.

Pair up your students and tell them that they will interview their partners before introducing them to the class. After they think of interview questions, they should write their suggestions on the chalkboard or on a piece of paper. Questions may relate to family members, pets, hobbies, sports, special possessions, and other areas of expertise. Suggest that interviewers take notes during the interview to help them recall information when they "present" their partners to the class. If you teach young children, you may want to invite upper grade students to act as interviewers and presenters. Be sure the interviewees get the interview notes from their partners for their "All About Me" folders.

Storytelling Festival.

After you distribute "Ideas for Storytelling" forms (*See Figure 4, on pg 21*), ask your students to check three topics about which they want to tell stories. Then, working in pairs, have your students exchange forms, interview each other about all three topics, and then select the one topic that the interviewee had most to say about. Next combine the pairs into groups of four and have each student retell the story he or she selected. The original partner may prompt the storyteller if necessary.

FIGURE 2

WHAT'S ON YOUR MIND?

Use the boxes above to write your ideas.

1. Describe something that you have kept for years because it has good memories for you.

2. Describe your favorite time of year.

3. Name something that you do well and something else that you are still learning to do.

4. Describe your favorite place to be alone.

Appeared in *Live Wire Classroom Ideas K-7.* NCTE August 1985

FIGURE 3

WHAT'S ON YOUR MIND?

Draw or write about the things, people and
events in your life that are important to you.

FIGURE 4

IDEAS FOR STORYTELLING

Please ask me about the three ideas I've checked:

_____ a special toy	_____ the things I collect
_____ my pet	_____ someone who is special to me
_____ what I'm good at	_____ what I'm afraid of
_____ the best party	_____ the worst party
_____ what I really like	_____ what I really can't stand
_____ a special place	_____ how I've changed
_____ what I'm most proud of	_____ what I'm sorry about
_____ my brother/sister	_____ someone I miss a lot
_____ my favorite time of year	_____ being jealous
_____ a first time experience	_____ a time I helped someone
_____ what moving was like	_____ being lost
_____ a special discovery	_____ a story someone told me
_____ my worst day	_____ my best day
_____ a scary experience	_____ what I did when I was little

My Ideas

_____ _____   _____ _____

_____ _____   _____ _____

Family Stories.

Send letters to parents *(See Figure 5, which follows.)* asking them to tell their child a family story that the child can retell to classmates. Suggest that your students ask questions and take notes or ask parents to write notes to help them remember important details. You may also want to invite the parents into the classroom as guest storytellers.

Another form of "Family Stories" is a family interview. Ask your students to brainstorm questions to ask one or more family members. For example, they could ask the following questions.

✦ What is your favorite food?

✦ What was your favorite book when you were young?

✦ What do you most enjoy doing when you have free time?

✦ What kind of work do you do?

✦ Did you ever have a nickname?

Duplicate the questions and send the interview forms and a cover letter home with each child. Parents of young children can help with the writing, but the children should ask the questions. Then have your students share the information with classmates.

Collections.

Invite those students who collect special things to display them in the classroom. (e.g., rocks, comic books, sea shells, stuffed animals, miniature cars, trading cards, and stamps.) Place small or fragile objects in clear, sealed bags so they don't get lost or broken. As part of the display, include index cards written by the collector telling a few important things everyone should know about the objects in the collection. Then give each collector a few minutes or so to talk about the collection and answer their classmates' questions.

Of course, guidelines for handling displayed materials should be set up in advance with the class, and sensitivity employed in situations where children may not be able to afford collections.

NOTEBOOK WRITING

As a result of sharing their personal interests and histories with classmates, my students realize that they have many important things to say about themselves and are, therefore, ready to move into notebook writing. A notebook provides practice for writing, and like tennis or skating, the more students write, the better they seem to get at it. I also distinguish notebooks from journals, which are nothing more than brief notes about daily routines and events. I use notebooks to encourage writing that is free-flowing and full of endless possibilities.

Students can use their notebooks as a source for writing project ideas. In their book, *Living Between the Lines*, Lucy Calkins and Shelley Harwayne show how teachers encourage reflective notebook writing and help their students craft promising entries into powerful stories.

Notebooks merit a careful and supportive introduction. I think it's helpful to students if you give them a clear written statement explaining notebook writing as well as your expectations. The letter on page 24 is the way I explain notebook writing to my students.

Try to saturate students with a variety of writing, thinking, reading, and discussing experiences that will make notebook writing natural and meaningful. You'll recognize the signs of real writers when students begin to write in their notebooks without being asked, or when you notice students rereading and marking entries in a search for language and themes that they will develop into an important writing project.

NOTEBOOK EXPLORATIONS

Although you may have explained notebook writing to your students they will need to see examples of a variety of entries and learn what notebooks mean to writers. The following four suggestions will help your students become familiar with notebooks and learn how to develop their own.

FIGURE 5

Dear Parents,

   Please help us with a language arts project. We would like to collect stories about family traditions, celebrations, events, or an interesting family member. If you have childhood memories about your own school and homelife or anecdotes about a family member who immigrated to America, we'd love to hear about that, too.

   Therefore, please tell your child a story about any one of these topics. I have asked all of my students to take notes after hearing their stories so they can remember the details when they share their family stories with their classmates.

                                        Sincerely,

Dear Student,

   This year you will keep a writing notebook in which you will record memories, thoughts, and feelings. Your notebook will be a place where you can play around with words and ideas and where you can write something without worrying about whether it's any good or not. However, there are a few things you should know about writing notebooks.

✦ Bring in any kind of notebook that you like as long as it has plenty of blank lined pages. You may cover your notebook with cloth, contact paper, wallpaper, a collage, or your own drawings. Decorate your notebook in a way that reflects you as a person; for example, if you are into sports or music, design a cover that shows this.

✦ Date each entry.

✦ Don't worry about spelling, but write clearly enough for me to understand what you've written. I will read your notebook, but you can keep a page private if you fold it over.

✦ You may write about wishes and dreams, but otherwise stick to real life. You'll have opportunities to write fiction later on this year.

✦ Reread your notebook frequently to look for strong images (word pictures). Later on, I will also show you how to look for and connect different entries that relate to similar subjects or ideas. You will probably find something important in your notebook that is worth developing during our writing workshops.

✦ You will have time to share these special entries with your classmates *if* you wish to.

Sincerely,

P.S. Take care of your notebook. It will become a treasure that you will want to keep forever.

Model Notebook Writing.

I usually begin by explaining the ways in which notebook writing differs from diary writing. For example, I tell my students that there are two ways I could record events about a shopping trip at the supermarket: diary entries and notebook entries. In a daily diary, I would record the date and give the bare facts of each day's event by writing such things as the following.

"Today is Tuesday. We had a fire drill in school. At 3:30 I went to the A & P to buy supplies for dinner. I did not have enough money so I just bought milk and tomatoes. I went home to get three dollars more. Then I went back to get the cookies. Had dinner, watched television and went to bed at eleven."

A notebook entry, on the other hand, is full of rich description of one significant experience or idea. If I were writing in a notebook, I would focus in some depth on only one of the experiences mentioned above. For examples, I might write the following.

"I had a really embarrassing moment yesterday. There I was at the checkout stand with only two containers of milk, four tomatoes, and two packages of Oreo cookies. I must have waited at least ten or fifteen minutes while people with heaping baskets of food were checked out. When it was my turn, the checkout clerk said, 'Seven dollars and twenty cents, please.'

I reached into my wallet and found only a five dollar bill. 'Oh, I know I had more than this,' I said. Then I went rummaging through my purse and my pockets. I could just feel everyone's eyes burning through me. My face felt red hot. Suddenly I remembered that I had given my son three dollars for lunch money that morning. I told the clerk I'd come back for the cookies later and couldn't wait to get out of that store. But my son loves Oreos so—would you believe it—I went back later and bought them. I guess I risked feeling embarrassed just to see him smile when I unpacked his favorite dessert. Of course, I didn't go back to the same check out counter."

I tell my students that a notebook page which says, "Today I went to the supermarket," isn't worth much to a writer, but a page full of word pictures and feelings could be developed and used in a story some day. If you teach upper grade students, have them experiment with diary and notebook writing styles. First ask them to write a "bare-bones" diary type of entry that tells a little about a lot of things. Then have them write a focused and detailed entry on a single subject or idea that relates to the diary entry.

Discuss Authors' Comments About Notebooks.

Using resource books, authors' memoirs, and professional journals, collect comments on notebook writing made by your students' favorite authors. Roald Dahl, an author my students like very much, wrote:

"I have had this book ever since I started trying to write seriously. There are ninety-eight pages in the book. I've counted them. And just about every one of them is filled up on both sides with these so-called story ideas...."
(Meet the Authors and Illustrators. Scholastic, 1991, p. 89)

Children familiar with the poetry of Eve Merriam are always delighted and surprised by comments of hers like the following.

"I always have a notebook, always...by my bed. I never travel, even to the post office without a notebook in my hand...I once got caught without a notebook and it was just painful for me to have to walk all the way home and do nothing but chant over those couple of words I had [in my head].
(The New Advocate, Summer 1989)

Jack Prelutsky's comments also show how important notebook entries are to him as a writer.

"I save all my ideas notebooks—I have at least fifty—and when I'm ready to write another book of poems I start working my way through all the notebooks...In my notebooks the ideas could be in the form

of a single nonsense word that I've made up or a few lines of rhyme that may be the beginning of a poem, or the end of one."
(*How Writers Write* by Pamela Lloyd. Heinemann, 1989)

Share Examples of Children's Notebook Entries.

After you ask your students to recall the kinds of subjects or topics their classmates have written about in their notebooks, list them on a chart or chalkboard. (*See examples of notebook entries in Figure 6 on pp. 28, 29.*)

Another good idea is to read aloud and discuss notebook entries written by fictional characters in children's books such as the following excerpt from *Harriet the Spy* by Louise Fitzhugh (Harper & Row, 1964). (Another example from *Anastasia Krupnik* by Lois Lowry is Figure 28 on page 108 in the Appendix.)

> *Harriet never goes anywhere without her notebook, but problems arise when her classmates discover that she has been writing about them. The sixth grader's notes are sometimes humorous, sometimes nasty, but always sharp and thoughtful. Here are some examples.*

Notes on people sitting in a train car:
> *Man with rolled white socks, fat legs. Woman with one cross-eye an a long nose. Horrible looking little boy and a fat blonde mother who keeps wiping his nose off. Funny lady looks like a teacher and is reading. I don't think I'd like to live where any of these people live or do the same things they do, I bet that little boy is sad and cries a lot. I bet that lady with the cross-eye looks in the mirror and just feels terrible. (pp. 13, 14)*

Notes made while daydreaming on her bed:
> *Maybe when I grow up I can have an office. On the door it can say "Harriet the Spy" in gold letters. And then it can have office hours like the dentist's door and underneath it can say* Any spy work

undertaken. *I guess I won't put the price on the door. Then they'll have to come in and ask me. I can go there every day from eleven to four and write in my notebook. People will come in and tell me who to go and spy on and I can do that outside of office hours. I wonder if I will get any murder cases. I would have to have a gun and follow people but I bet it would be at night and I wouldn't be allowed out. (pp. 65, 66)*

Notes made after a good friend goes away:
> *I feel all the same things when I do things alone as when Ole Golly was here. The bath feels hot, the bed feels soft, but I feel there's a funny little hole in me that wasn't there before, like a splinter in your finger, but this is somewhere above my stomach. (pp.108, 109)*

Demonstrate How to Choose a Notebook.

If your students make their own notebooks, they will begin to take pride in their notebooks—even before writing in them. You may want to begin by displaying several notebooks in different sizes, shapes, and materials. Then discuss reasons for individual preferences; for instance, you might say that some will prefer a spiral notebook because it's convenient to turn everything back under the page they're writing on. Others, however, might select a small notebook because they can carry it easily from place to place. A soft cover looseleaf notebook, on the other hand, not only offers more space on a page for writing, but it allows writers to insert pages that they've written at home.

I would also encourage your students to decorate the covers of their notebooks with words, drawings, cut out pictures, fabric, or contact paper in a way that reflects their personalities. A football fan, for example, might write, draw, or paste on a cover pictures of a favorite player, game tickets, trading cards, and football terms.

The more students can personalize their notebooks, the more ownership of their writing they will feel.

SPRINGBOARDS FOR NOTEBOOK WRITING

Once your students are familiar with notebooks and have selected one, they will need some help from you to begin filling the blank pages. One way to get them started, for example, is to ask them to brainstorm a variety of possibilities for notebook entries and then chart their suggestions. Be sure to encourage them to explore additional possibilities that they can add to the chart. Another good way to get notebook writing going is through prompts or sentence stems such as one of the following.

✦ A place I like is...

✦ I was really proud when...

✦ If I had three wishes...

✦ I hated it when...

✦ I'll never forget...

✦ My favorite...

After trying out and sharing some notebook topics and prompts, your students will be ready to use some of the following twelve open-ended strategies in order to fill notebook pages with their ideas. As you go over each of the following strategies, ask your students to list them in their notebooks. Then, if possible, give them ten minutes or so each day to experiment with the different strategies. Once they are comfortable with them, then encourage them to create other strategies of their own.

Dip into the "All About Me" Folder.

The following projects, crafts, and games already described in this chapter will provide ideas for notebook entries.

✦ an interest inventory

✦ photographs

✦ a time line

✦ notes made for family stories

✦ scavenger hunt index cards

✦ family interviews

✦ an IDEAS FOR STORYTELLING form

✦ a WHAT'S ON YOUR MIND? form

✦ index cards describing collections

Practice Visualizing.

List feeling words such as the following on a chart: *happy, sad, proud, frightened, embarrassed, angry.* Then ask your students to choose a feeling that they remember experiencing by saying something such as, "Close your eyes and relax. Think for a few minutes about the time you felt that way. In your mind try to picture the place where you were. Imagine that you're back there. (pause) Keeping your eyes closed, look around carefully. (pause) What do you see? (pause) What do you hear? (pause) Who else is there? (pause) What's happening? (pause) What are you thinking?" If you teach young children, you may want to suggest that they draw the visualized scene before writing about it.

Do Fast Writing.

Fast writing, or free writing, is a never-fail technique to get anyone to write. It works particularly well after a visualizing experience. However, you'll need to give your students the following guidelines in advance.

1. I will set a timer for seven minutes.

2. When I say "go," begin writing immediately whatever comes to your mind. Don't worry about spelling, handwriting, sentences, or even sticking to your topic.

3. Keep your pencil moving on your page. Don't stop for anything (except a fire drill). Don't stop to erase or read what you've written.

4. If you get stuck, write the last word you've written over and over until a new thought comes.

5. Stop when the time is up. Shake out your writing hand and read what you've written. Look for surprises by underlining any vivid images and strong feelings.

Observe It Close Up.

Give your students index cards with a small hole in each one. Suggest they look through the hole to focus on their clothing, sneaker, hand, chair, or any other object on or inside their desk. Have them look for the smallest details—such as designs, lines, colors, shapes, markings—and record their

FIGURE 6

STUDENT NOTEBOOK ENTRIES

#1

I wish that the world was flat and Columbus was wrong and Magellen fell off the Earth and is still living on Mars. I wish that Vespucii discovered Canada and Cartir discoverd United States and Sir Francis Drake fell off Earth too and landed on Pluto and if you go visit Pluto you would see him with tons and tons of winter coats on and still shivering. I wish Champlain discoverd Greenland and Pocahontas helped Balboa. I wish Vasco De Gama traveled with Ponce De Leon and Bart Simpson was a famous explorer.

John, Grade 4

#2

My Wallpaper (How it looks)

Three different kinds of boats fill the wall.
   Along with a sailer steering a ship.
   Anchors and cannons take up the spots were boats and sailers miss
   One big diagram of a ship overlapping a lantern you can hardly see.
   But what I like best is the drawing of me my little sister did on the wall.

Danny, Grade 5

3

Why, why won't my parents have a baby
I hate math

Jillian, Grade 4

STUDENT NOTEBOOK ENTRIES

#4

Corn Fever

Dinner's ready called my mom, I asked what is it. "corn!
                                        Corn!!!
I was really horrified!!
is there something else I asked No answer my mother, so I had to eat it.
      That night I got fever I have———
CORNFEVER
I screamed!

                                        Stuti, Grade 4

#5

I rember when I was little. I thoght there was a little brown blob of a monster smaller than me with a fat little wierd tail that would get me if I didn't go to bed or take a bath. Whenever I used to take a bath I would ask my dad to make the water really cold then I would dump all of my toys in the tub, which was quite alot. I would hop in and My dad would say "be careful some pengins might come."

                                        Christine, Grade 4

6

My kitchen. Warm and small. Huge plants covering the room. Sunlight pours throught the windows. The walls are painted light Blue. There are some blotches of white. It looks like a forest with a blue sky. I sometimes sleep there and it feels like sleeping in a forest. The windows pour in darkness so the paint looks dark blue. I like it there alot. When we play tag I hide in there so no one sees me. And if I want to have a snack the kitche[n]s right next to me. I might make my room there except it be to small. I think of it as my secret forest. My friends or cousins (My Korean friends) they think it is a small inaproprieat room. But I think it's a forest.

                                        Jae, Grade 5

observations. Close observation also works well outdoors in a field or on the playground where there are plants, trees, rocks, insects, and other natural points of interest.

Another good way to help your students develop a writer's keen eye for small details is to ask them to write while looking at people, animals, objects, or places. Emphasize the importance of looking at familiar subjects as if they had never seen them before. You may want to read aloud a notebook entry that describes a person or read the following excerpt from Virginia Hamilton's poem that describes a place.

> *Our house is two stories high shaped like a white box. There is a yard stretched around it and in back a wooden porch. Under the back porch is my place. I rest there. I go there when I have to be alone. It is always shaded and damp. Sunlight only slants through the slats in long strips of light, and the smell of the damp is moist green, like the moss that grows there....*
> *In Home.* (HarperCollins, 1992)

Use Your "Listening Ear"
Open the classroom windows and doors and remind your students that they need to be very quiet in order to capture barely perceptible sounds and words.

Make Lists
After you tell your students about Anastasia Krupnik's THINGS I LOVE/THINGS I HATE lists, have them brainstorm in their notebooks for additional ideas for list making. Afterwards, ask them to share their ideas. Following are some ideas my students have suggested.
+ Favorite Words
+ Sayings
+ Favorite Foods
+ Songs
+ Games
+ Things I See on the Walls
+ Things Inside My Desk
+ Things I Have to Do
+ Things My Parents Always Say

+ Things I Want for My Birthday

Give Four Reasons Why
Ask your students to think of something— anything— that they want to see happen— such as a longer recess. Once they have told what it is, they should give four reasons why it should happen.

Use the News
Even students who are too young to read newspapers hear and wonder about things that are happening in the world around them. You might read aloud an appropriate news article to younger children and demonstrate how you would write your reaction to it. If you teach upper grade students, ask them to clip out interesting news articles and paste them into their notebooks for reflection, or you may want to tape a segment from a televised news report for their reaction.

Write a Letter
Often writing seems to flow more easily for students when they have someone in mind as an audience for their ideas and opinions. Therefore, ask your students to pretend they are writing a letter to someone because they have something to tell that person. "Pretending" to write frees them to consider any recipient of any message—such as the President, the principal, someone they secretly admire, and/or a family member or friend. Tell your students that the letter may be one they decide to send, or it may be a message that they would never want delivered.

Tell How to Do Something
Explain that everyone is an expert in certain areas—whether it's making something (a cake, a sand castle, a paper hat) or doing something (playing baseball, drawing cartoons, finding lost objects, baby sitting). Discuss with your students what it means to be an expert, and lead them to see that they too are experts in certain fields. Ask your students to explain what they do well and how they do it. (One thing most children do better than adults is to program a VCR or play a video game.)

THE USE OF PICTURE BOOKS AS MODELS

Picture books are a wonderful resource for writers of all ages. Jim Trelease, author of *The Read Aloud Handbook* says, "The picture book should be on the reading list of every child in every grade through twelve years of school." Many picture books use precise and beautiful language and portray situations and themes that are meaningful to young people. For notebook writing, I try to select picture books that will stimulate memories of people, places, and events. If you are going to use picture books to stimulate notebook writing for the first time, my own experiences may help you see how a few of these books led fourth graders to express their own ideas of real and imaginary places.

I begin by reading aloud beautifully written picture books that impart a strong sense of place—such as Crescent Dragonwagon's *Home Place*, a kind of story/poem, (MacMillan, 1990), Anna Egan Smucker's *No Star Nights*, (Knopf, 1989) and *Home* (HarperCollins, 1992), an anthology of essays and poems by 13 well-known authors of children's books.

Following such a reading recently, my students and I talked about the author's use of language, recalling lines and words we liked. When I asked my students to write in their notebooks, I urged them to use vivid word pictures and beautiful language just as the authors of the picture books had done. The fourth graders wrote without stopping for several minutes, and their results really surprised me. Their writing was livelier than any of their earlier entries. Following are a few excerpts from this group of fourth graders.

Charlie

I like to go to the top of the mountain because it feels like I'm on top of the world seeing everything...When you're going down the steepest slope all the snow is blowing in your face. It's like diving into a big glass or tub but you don't get wet unless you fall. Then at the bottom of the mountain big bumps come on. I jump and when I'm in the air I feel like I just jumped off an airplane. I can't wait to go back up the mountain.

Kelly

It was a windy fall day to walk home from school. The leaves blew mad in our face as my friend and I struggled to get indoors. On the way home whenever we saw a hudge pile of racked up leaves we ran! Ohhhh how we ran. As we flew in to the pillow and were both drowning each other in the leaves we were silent, then we knew what was in each others mind as my neighbor's dog flew out the door and into the bushes....

Scott

I'd like to be in a treehouse, A treehouse in Hawaii, a cocunut tree. The steps you'd take to get to the treehouse would be fine Dogwood bark. Smoothed out and polished. When the sun would set it would make another sun on the steps. The treehouse would be nailed together with brown nails... There would be one plank of wood missing. This way I could look out and see the ocean. I'd have four cocunuts lined up on a gleaming bench. I'd bring up a hammer to crack the cocunuts for milk. I'd go through one cocunut a day. Sometimes when I look out the missing plank.I see far-away ships with masts bold and bright. And I'd have a cannon at my side with 10 cannon balls leaning against my feet. I'd hear the shout of "Land Ho" or "Ships approaching at 3 'o clock." Then I'd fire a cannonball and "Boom" it would explode. Sending the ship into flames...

SUGGESTIONS FOR PICTURE BOOKS

Following is a short list of additional picture books that invite notebook writing. Of course, there are many, many others you can explore on your own. I suggest that you keep a changing collection in your classroom to provide pleasure and serve as resources for teaching your students about good writing.

Family

Granpa by John Burningham (Crown, 1984).

The Patchwork Quilt by Valerie Flurney (Dial, 1985).

My Great Aunt Arizona by Gloria Houston (Harper Collins, 1992).

Always Grandma by Vaunda Michaux Nelson (Putnam, 1988).

When I Was Young in the Mountains by Cynthia Rylant (Dutton, 1982).

When the Relatives Came by Cynthia Rylant (Bradbury Press, 1985).

Feelings and Growing Pains

Chrysanthenum by Kevin Henkes (Greenwillow, 1991).

Amazing Grace by Mary Hoffman (Dial, 1991).

Birthday Presents by Cynthia Rylant (Lothrop, Lee, Shepard, 1987).

Alexander and the Terrible, Horrible, No-Good, Very Bad Day by Judith Viorst (Atheneum, 1972).

If I Were in Charge of the World and other Worries by Judith Viorst (MacMillan, 1984)

Earrings by Judith Viorst (Atheneum, 1990).

Ira Sleeps Over by Bernard Waber (Houghton Mifflin, 1972).

Someday by Charlotte Zolotow (Harper Collins, 1989).

Survival and Courage

How Many Days to America? by Eve Bunting (Clarion Books, 1988)

Gooseberries to Oranges by B. Cohen (Lothrop, Lee & Shepard, 1982).

Tight Times by Barbara Hazen (Puffin Books, 1983).

Knots on a Counting Rope by Bill Martin Jr. and John Archambault (Holt, 1987).

The Ghost Eye Tree by Bill Martin Jr. (Holt, 1985).

The Rag Coat by Lauren Mills (Little, Brown, 1991).

Hurricane by David Weisner (Clarion, 1990).

Dark and Full of Secrets by Carol Carrick (Clarion, 1984).

STRATEGIES FOR USING PICTURE BOOKS

After each reading, discuss vivid images and powerful language used by the author. Then have your students share stories about personal memories the story evoked. Following are some additional strategies for notebook writing when your students read picture books on their own.

Match a Memory to the Story

After reading aloud a story, tell your students about a personal memory that the story brought to your mind. Then ask them to write their own memory of a person, place, or experience. Remind them to create word pictures and beautiful language just as the author did.

Quote the Author

Have your students look for lines in the story worth remembering and then copy them into their notebooks. If they wish, they could even write or draw something inspired by that quote.

THE POSSIBILITIES IN NOTEBOOK ENTRIES

Show your students how to look through their notebooks for meaningful entries, entries that focus on the same subject or theme and on entries that include vivid descriptions. You may want to collect and read the notebooks yourself at this point in order to help them make their decisions, or you can give your students several questions such as the following to keep in mind as they reread their notebook entries.

✦ What do you notice in your writing? Which entries seem to stand out?

✦ Is there one idea or subject that you seem to write about more than any other?

✦ Which entries show something important about you?

✦ Which entry or entries tell about someone or something that matters a lot to you?

✦ Which entry or entries have the most beautiful or powerful language?

The following anecdotes and examples will give you an idea of what your students may find in their notebooks and the kinds of writing projects they can lead to.

Kelly (*grade 4*)

As an example of powerful language, Kelly selected the notebook entry that appears on page 00. First she read aloud and discussed her use of the following vivid word pictures with several of her classmates.

- ✦ "the leaves blew mad in our face..."
- ✦ "Whenever we saw a hudge pile of racked up leaves we ran! Ohhhh how we ran."
- ✦ "As we flew into the pillow and were both drowning each other in the leaves we were silent"

Because her images and language flowed so naturally, Kelly had a good start on a narrative essay. She added more information, created an ending and a title, and, of course, edited her work.

Johanna (*grade 2*)

Looking for several entries on the same subject, Johanna discovered three consecutive entries about a "game" or practical joke that she and her cousins had played on her mother. Following is her first entry.

> *"On Sunday My cousins came to celebrate my Grand Mothers Birthday. We played some games one of The games we were Kidnappers.*
>
> *We Kidnaped My baby sister and sent a Ranson note and it said. We are holding your dawter Evelyn for ranson for 1 rasberry + strawbery fruit rolls. Leave Them on The Mantale By The Christmus tree at 3.55*
>
> *Dont Look Back? Go Strait to The Kitchen.*
>
> *PS sined, Hungrey*
>
> *If it is not there you will pay!"*

Johanna's next two entries built up a complete story that ended with the return of her baby sister in exchange for the fruit rolls. When Johanna read the series of entries

aloud to her classmates, they urged her to "publish" the story.

Johanna's teacher photocopied the entries for her to use as a first draft. Johanna's entries were so detailed and complete that all she had to do to publish her story was to proofread and write the final copy of her personal narrative.

Sally (*grade 5*)

Sally found several notebook entries that focused on her older sister Kate. In a conference with her teacher, Sally explained that she'd like to write a picture storybook about Kate because she was "special." Despite the fact that she had written in some length about Kate, Sally drew only a few ideas for her picture book from the following entry.

> *"My sister Kate has blond shoulder leghth hair. She has blue eyes and she's the nicest person I ever met. I know your thinking no way. She's your sister how can she be the nicest person you've met but that's true. first of all she practicly raised me all by herself! and she taught me French and a lot of songs and she's always away at collage so we can't get on each others nerves she knows french as if the lived three quarters of her life in France!!! and she just learned Greek she gets good grades and she's 19 almost 20."*

Instead of "lifting" all or most of the story out of notebook entries for her writing project as Johanna and Kelly had, Sally selected only a few small details—the French and singing lessons—as idea seeds. Then she fleshed out these episodes and added several more that focused on the central theme of her notebook writings—growing up with a loving sister.

I do have some words of caution. First, be patient; don't expect all of your students to find a promising topic in their notebooks early in the year. Second, while ideas and language may grow out of your students' notebooks, the move from entry to writing project will usually involve them in the crafting and reshaping of ideas and words. Chapters 3 and 4 will show you how to help your students write their way into their first story of the year.

Questions Teachers Ask About Notebook Writing

Q Should notebook writing be done at home or only in class? I find that writing sometimes is lost when it leaves the classroom.

A That's true, but it's so important for students to have their notebooks at hand to capture fleeting thoughts and the sights and sounds around them. Youngsters who think of their notebooks as something special and valuable are also not likely to lose them. On the other hand, you may want young children or students who always tend to lose things to have two notebooks: one for home and one for school.

Q How often should I read my students' notebooks and what response, if any, should I make?

A It's a good idea to collect notebooks about every three weeks so that you can help your students look for a theme emerging out of their entries. In order to keep from feeling overwhelmed, you might want to call for the notebooks of a third of your class each week. Many teachers I know, particularly those who teach young children, maintain a written dialogue with them on the notebook pages. I use a "Post-it" type of sticky paper to mark particular pages for discussion in a notebook conference with a particular student. I also tab entries that include powerful images and feelings and encourage those writers to share them.

Q What should I do about bad language and negative comments about teachers and classmates?

A I tell my students that they can write anything they want to write in their notebooks; however, they cannot share entries with bad language or comments that might offend others in the class or in the school.

Q How do I evaluate notebook writing?

A I first observe how many entries were generated—especially during the initial focus on notebook writing. Of course, once students move into crafting a piece of writing, I would expect to see fewer entries. Fullness is another important quality to look for in entries. Are ideas, observations, and feelings pursued in some depth, or are most of the entries only brief jottings? I also look for signs of experimentation and diversity among the types of entries. Were there attempts to write poems, bits of overheard conversation, anecdotes, reflections, opinions, memories, and other diverse writings?

Q Should my students keep two separate notebooks—one for writing and another for responding to the books they have read?

A Separate notebooks make it easier for *me* to focus on reading at one time and writing at another. However, the occasional mix–up makes me realize how natural the combination (reading and writing) really is. Danny, for example, who wrote about the book *Fencing Is for Me*, described what he learned from the book that he could apply to improve his own fencing skills. That was a wonderful topic for a writing project!

CHAPTER THREE

Getting Ready to Launch the Writing Workshop

If I have learned one thing as a teacher of writing, it is that there is no standardized formula—no simple sequence of steps to follow—that will help children improve their writing. The good news is that there is a general plan that works for many teachers, and you have already learned how to use two important "keys" for making that plan work. The first key is a thoughtful organization of time, materials, space, and routines for your writing workshops. The second key to improving writing is the establishment of a comfortable and risk-free environment in which your students can begin to express and gather ideas in writing notebooks. Now you are ready for the third key—engaging your students in the process of writing.

MEETING WRITERS' NEEDS

An abundance of research on writing conducted over the years has helped me formulate the following philosophical framework that I think of as the student writer's Bill of Rights.

TIME

Here it is again—probably the single issue that teachers struggle with most often, but one that is absolutely crucial to helping students become good writers. When I consider my own writing process—the way I go about formulating ideas—writing, analyzing, rewriting, analyzing again, more rewriting, and then finally polishing, I realize the importance of giving students lots of time to write, and I believe without a doubt that time to write is time well spent. The composing, sharing, and revising processes also allow students to practice critical thinking strategies and to reinforce speaking and reading skills—all in a meaningful context.

OWNERSHIP

Youngsters who are encouraged to write about things they know and care about develop a confidence that sustains them as they work for weeks to improve their writing. Ownership also means that students have a high degree of control over the decisions that all writers must make while they go about planning and revising their work. When my students reject suggestions I have made in favor of their own ideas, I congratulate myself for empowering them to think for themselves.

RESPONSE

Because student writers need frequent, positive feedback, I try to receive each work with respect—no matter how good or bad I think it is. Faced with blunt criticism or a dour expression, most students (and adult writers, too!) wilt and lose interest in developing their writing. As a result, a natural and friendly conversational tone goes a long way in encouraging writers to develop or rework a piece.

DEMONSTRATION

Adult and student models are important to young writers. Whenever I want my students to move into a different writing mode—notebook writing, for example—or learn a new technique, I model the process for them and sometimes provide them with examples written by other students. Because it's also important for students to see that I value writing for myself, I keep a notebook for reflecting on my teaching.

PURPOSE

I let my students know that writing is meant for more than filling a portfolio or pleasing me because writing should affect the student's real world. Songs, essays, stories, poems, and plays can move and entertain. Letters and news articles can persuade and inform. Manuals or handbooks can instruct. Helping students find a purpose and audience for a work motivates them to give it their best efforts.

FEATURES OF INTRODUCTORY WORKSHOPS

There are many ways to get your students to write. Some teachers tell about an event in their own lives that might make a good story. Others suggest that students find topics by looking through their notebooks, interest surveys, profile drawings, and other self-discovery activities. Still others find that students are eager to write after fellow students have read interesting personal narratives aloud.

Following is a description of another approach, one that accomplishes three things simultaneously: (1) it engages students in the writing process, (2) it teaches them about good writing, and (3) it builds a lasting framework for writing. The four significant features of my introductory workshops are as follows.

- ✦ Demonstrations and mini-lessons
- ✦ Reference charts
- ✦ Writing and sharing
- ✦ Conferences

DEMONSTRATIONS AND MINI-LESSONS

I remember how nervous I felt when I first shared my writing with students. I was afraid they would see how awful it was. Instead, they loved hearing about my experience during a minor earthquake in California. It was the story that mattered, I discovered, not my writing. When I talked about my recollections of an incident, someone always suggested that I "put that part in." The truth is that talking to my students and responding to their questions really did help me improve my story! More importantly, though, my writing demonstrations help youngsters understand the writer's process, some criteria for good writing, and the importance of response.

During six days of demonstrations (of course, the students have more days than that to work on their writing), I model the various stages of my process of writing from brainstorming a topic to proofreading. Taking into account the questions and suggestions of my students, I revise my draft each evening. The next day, as I share my revisions, I give them the reasons for my choices.

When I contemplate making changes in my draft, I let the children hear me think aloud. A "think-aloud" is a simple but remarkable teaching tool. It makes strategic thinking visible in a non-directive way. As a result, my students develop a real feeling for the nature of the process and the revision strategies that writers use. They also see how their questions and comments quite naturally lead me to make changes that improve my writing. Besides helping my students understand the process a writer goes through, the demonstrations "teach" basic criteria for good writing—such as a unifying focus, specific details, interesting leads, and

satisfying endings.

In addition, I mean, I want my students to know how a writer *feels*. For instance, I talk about how hard it is to reveal parts of my life to others and how some responses to my draft make me feel good about myself as a writer while "bossy" comments do not.

REFERENCE CHARTS

Reference charts help to keep writing workshops running smoothly. Developing a piece of writing entails a great many strategies and activities that students can follow if you take them apart and outline them in small, manageable bites. Therefore, at the beginning of the year, my students often look to these charts for guidance until they internalize their own process for writing. For example, on the first reference chart WHAT WRITERS DO (*See Figure 19 on page 99.*) I record—in the students' own words—the strategies I modeled that day. By the end of the six demonstrations, the chart outlines the writing process from brainstorming to recopying the edited piece.

As the demonstrations continue, my students help me develop additional reference charts. (When teaching upper elementary or middle school students, I also provide them with individual copies of the charts for their work-in-progress writing folders.) However, I make sure that my students and I always generate the following reference charts during the introductory workshops.

- ✦ HOW TO FIND A TOPIC (*See Figure 18 on page 98.*)
- ✦ WHAT WRITERS DO (*See Figure 19 on page 99.*)
- ✦ WHAT TO DO WHEN YOU ARE STUCK (*See Figure 20 on page 100.*)
- ✦ HOW TO HELP A WRITER (*See Figure 21 on page 101.*)
- ✦ MARKS FOR REVISING AND EDITING (*See Figure 22 on page 102.*)
- ✦ AM I READY TO EDIT? (*See Figure 23 on page 103.*)
- ✦ EDITING STEPS (*See Figures 24 and 25 on pages 104 and 105.*)

◆ POSSIBLE WAYS TO PUBLISH (*See Figure 26 on page 106.*)

WRITING AND SHARING

Each day after my demonstration lesson is completed, my students begin to write. I ask them to approximate the process I demonstrated, but I assure them that their writing does not have to keep pace with mine. Beginning on the third day, I take a quick survey of their writing plans to assess their progress. (*See Figure 27 on page 107.*)

Because writing is hard work and takes a lot of energy, I'm never surprised when some students run out of steam rather quickly. They'll say they can't think of anything more to write or tell me they have finished by writing "THE END" after half a page. Of course, as soon as I find time to confer with them, they will talk about their ideas and discover they really do have more to write. The gap between the time they stop writing and the time they receive help, of course, is crucial. Paper airplanes fly and lines of frustrated writers trail behind me if I don't give youngsters strategies for working independently. Some teachers solve this problem by asking their students to read a book while waiting for assistance, but I like to keep them in the writing mode by providing several options for blocked writers. (*You will find these options in Figure 20,* WHAT TO DO WHEN YOU ARE STUCK *on page 100.*)

Sharing right from the start what students have written is very important. The reaction of classmates gives a writer direction in developing or revising a piece. Sometimes the benefits extend to class members who learn effective writing techniques from the student who is sharing. Before the first sharing session, my students talk about how important it is to give the writer specific feedback. Instead of just saying, "That was good," my students learn to let the writer know the line or part they liked and why they think it's good. If there are parts they don't understand, they ask the writer for more information. My students' responses to a writer always improve throughout the year as they listen to the kinds of questions I ask during conferences and sharing time.

CONFERENCES

Conferences help to drive the writing process. Students need to talk about what they will write about before they actually sit down to write, and they often require on-going feedback through different draft stages as they try to make their meaning clear. Conferring is, in fact, my main responsibility during a workshop. By giving students access to writing materials and strategies for dealing with writing blocks, I free myself to work with individuals and small groups. Therefore, in the introductory workshops, my students receive response to their writing in a variety of ways: with a partner, with me, and with a group.

THE PARTNER CONFERENCE

As soon as my students have generated at least a few ideas or topics that they think they might want to write about, a partner conference can take place. By getting the reaction of their partners to their stories, they are better able to determine which story their readers will ultimately be able to picture most clearly and which they will think is most important. Partner conferences are also extremely useful for editing, and they work well for helping writers choose titles, beginnings, and endings. My students find that the following guidelines give them help and direction when they conduct their partner conferences.

◆ Sit in a conference area where you won't disturb others.

◆ Talk in low voices.

◆ Ask the writer what he or she needs help with.

◆ Listen to the writer read or talk.

◆ Respond to the writer's problem. Ask questions and make some suggestions.

◆ Be helpful, but not bossy. Say, "You might want to try this. . . or this. . ." Don't say,

"You should. . ."

✦ Keep conference short—under seven minutes.

✦ End conference by asking the writer what he or she plans to do next.

THE TEACHER/STUDENT CONFERENCE

Although I sometimes meet with individual students at a conference table, I usually circulate around the room, going from student to student for brief conferences. The chart WHAT TO DO WHEN YOU ARE STUCK helps those students who are don't know how to proceed work independently while they wait for me. (*See Figure 20 on page 100.*)

I may simply ask a writer, "How's it going?" and take my lead from the student's response, or after quickly skimming a page, I might say, "Oh, I see you're writing about the time your sister was born. You say she was cute. I wonder how she actually looked." After listening to the writer's description, I suggest she find a way to include those visual details. (*See page 62 for an example of a one-to-one conference.*)

Usually I can reach 10 to 14 students for individual conferences in 40 minutes. I then collect the writing of the remaining students and let them know that I plan to read their work and meet with them the next day. Writing one or two questions on "Post-its" and sticking them onto the drafts prepares me for each conference.

THE GROUP CONFERENCE

In group conferences, I act as a conference facilitator, but it is input from all group members that actually helps students improve their writing. Several chairs are permanently placed around the conference table as an open invitation for students to join the group. As one student leaves, another may take his or her place. Sometimes, however, after reviewing writing folders, I invite to the table a few students who haven't been up to the table for a while and, therefore, could benefit from the group's response. Group conferences usually give the

participants an opportunity to read their writing all the way through. The following conference format helps my students deal with writing problems while allowing them to retain control over their work.

1. Because a writer usually has an agenda, the conference often begins when someone in the group asks the writer, "What do you think you may need some help with? If, however a writer simply says, "Is this good?" or "I'm stuck," the others in the group should encourage the writer to think about more specific needs—such as finding a title, an ending, or more information, and, perhaps, determining whether a certain part makes sense. Once the writer identifies a need, he or she should then discuss the piece or read from a draft while the others in the group offer various suggestions and options.

2. The responders should always contribute to the agenda. If they don't understand something in the piece, they should ask the writer about it. At this point, however, I discourage students from asking "picky" questions that require brief answers. For example, I suggest they save a question like "What was that boy's name?" for an editing conference. Instead I recommend that they ask "how" and "why" kinds of questions that encourage the writer to talk more. The responders should also try to draw out information about visual images, opinions, and feelings and then give the writer plenty of time to think about a response to their questions.

3. Because the responders need to listen while the writer does the talking, it's the voice of the writer that should be heard more than any other in a conference. I also use body language—such as leaning toward the writer and focusing intently—to model the importance of giving the writer complete attention.

4. Toward the end of the conference, one of the responders should begin to help the writer remember what was said by saying something such as, "You've given us a

much clearer picture. Listen to some of the things you told us." Then the other members of the group should take turns "playing back" the writer's own words.

5. At the end of a conference, a responder should ask, "How do you think you might use the information you've just talked about? or "What do you think you'll do next?" Although writers now should have a clear idea of what they will write, some young children may still be uncertain about where or how to insert the new information. As a result, they need to be assured that after writing something, they can have another conference to figure out where it belongs.

After receiving the group's response, the writer should leave the conference table, making room for someone else to join the group. Of course, time usually runs out before all of the students at the conference table have had a chance to discuss their writing. Those writers who do not have a chance to meet with a group should have the opportunity to get feedback from the whole class during sharing time that same day or meet with their teacher the following day.

RESPONSES DURING CONFERENCES

If you are venturing into this area of conferences for the first time, keep in mind that learning how to respond to writing takes time. For a start, ask yourself a few basic questions—such as the following—when hearing or reading a draft. (I have also included a few examples of my comments and questions to students.)

1. **Is there sufficient meaning and information to make the piece interesting?**

   "I think you have the beginning of an interesting idea here. Why did you decide to write about this? Why is it important to you?"

   "When you think back to this ____, what do you remember? Why was it so special?"

   "You seem to be onto something here. Can

   you tell me more about it?"

   "I'd love to know more about   . Could you teach me something about it?"

2. **Is the writing visual? Are the details specific?**

   "You say you were feeling (mad, scared, happy, sad). If I had been there, how would I have known you felt that way?"

   "You say ____ looked (cute, funny, nice, pretty, weird). Try to describe ____ so that I can get a better picture in my mind."

   "What did you do when that happened?"

   "If I were right there with you, what would I have seen and heard?"

3. **Is the writing focused around a unifying idea or topic, or is the topic too broad?**

   Are there any parts that don't belong? (*See pages 44–45 for more information about focused writing.*)

   "It looks as though you discuss a lot of different things. I wonder what a table of contents might look like if you divided this piece into chapters? Which items or sections do you think would be the most important ones?"

   "What's the main thing you're trying to write about? Here's a part that doesn't seem to have much to do with that idea. Can you tell me how it connects to your main idea, or do you think you should leave it out?"

4. **Is the writing clear and understandable?**

   "I'm having trouble understanding this part. Can you say it another way?"

   "I'm not sure I know what you mean here. Could you help me understand it?"

   "How would you explain this to someone who has absolutely no knowledge of   ?"

5. **Is the writing organized with an interesting introduction, a logical sequence of ideas or events, and a satisfying ending?**

"I'm wondering whether you might find another way to introduce your story so it will grab a reader's interest."

"I wonder what it would sound like if you began your story a bit further down in the piece—maybe where you've written this interesting dialogue or this part where you show some action."

"Help me understand the order in which these things happened? Tell me what happened first, second, and so on."

"Is there an ending that could tie up the whole story? For example, when you think back on this experience, what feelings do you have about it now?"

"What message or opinion do you want to give someone who reads this? Did you learn any lesson as a result of your experience?"

6. **Does the writer's voice shine through with a sense of honesty and individuality?** (*The ability to write with voice develops over time as writers learn how to use words to express real thoughts and feelings. You will find an example of voice in a sixth grader's writing piece in Chapter 5 on page 63.*)

"If you were telling this part to your friend, how would you describe it?"

"What did you feel like saying when this happened? What were you thinking to yourself at the time?"

"You really showed me your feelings when you talked about this part, but I'm not sure I see it in your writing. How can you get more of yourself into your story?"

CONFERENCE MANAGEMENT

Conferences are actually opportunities for diagnosing writing problems and leading students—through talk and discussion—to find solutions to their own problems. If you teach a large class and are wondering how you can manage to help all of your students learn to write, you may want to consider some of the following strategies.

1. During the introductory workshops, plan additional time for all-class sharing conferences so that more students can receive response. All-class conferences help everyone learn something important about good writing—not just the students who are sharing.

2. Collect and review several writing folders each day. Then confer briefly with those writers individually on the following day while the other students are engaged in a quiet activity. You should conduct group conferences, however, as usual during workshop time.

3. Have more partner conferences after students gain some experience and understanding about what makes writing good. Some kind of response from a friendly reader is usually helpful to a writer and is certainly better than none at all.

To prepare your students for these early partner conferences, conduct a conference with a student while everyone else in the class observes, listens and, if possible, takes notes. You also should make a chart of student generated conference strategies that your students suggest. (*See pages 62 and 63 for additional partner conference guidelines.*) Then encourage any students who participate in effective partner conferences to reenact their discussion for the class. Ask the writer to show or describe the changes or revisions that resulted from a partner's feedback.

After the introductory workshops have taken your students through the writing process, they will be ready to publish their writing—but not necessarily at the same time because some will return to notebook writing while others will continue to require conferences. Because some students will move from notebooks to writing projects and others will move from published pieces into notebooks, you will find it increasingly easier to meet your students' conference needs.

Chapter 4 "Putting It All Together: Teaching Writing" will give you a close-up look at several workshops and help you guide your students through their first experience with the writing process.

Questions Teachers Ask
About Launching a Writing Workshop

Q You suggest letting students decide what they will write and how they will write. How can I do this when my students need to write on the same subject for their social studies and science reports?

A You can give your students choice in content area writing by breaking down the broad subjects they have studied into specific, individual topics. One way to do this is by constructing a graphic organizer. Write the main subject in a box or circle on the chalkboard. Then ask your students to brainstorm topics and sub-topics while you record them in smaller boxes or circles around the main subject. Invite your students to select the topic that most interests them or one that they know most about. Then suggest that they construct individual graphic organizers to identify sub-topics for their own area of interest.

Q When you circulate among students for individual conferences, don't your discussions distract other students who are trying to write?

A While it is true that students at nearby desks will occasionally stop writing to listen in on a conference, their time is not being wasted. I believe these impromptu "mini-lessons" teach the writer —as well as those sitting nearby—something important about good writing or a writer's process.

Q When I meet with one group of students, I can see a few other students talking at their desks instead of writing. Pretty soon, the classroom is so noisy!

A Interaction with classmates gives students new insights and may help them solve their writing problems. But when students' talk turns from a soft buzz to distracting noise, use the following strategies.

1. Be sure that your students know their options for independent work if they get stuck and can't continue writing. (*See Figure 20 on page 100.*)
2. Discontinue the group conference and circulate among students for brief, individual conferences.
3. You may need to set aside additional secluded areas for peer conferences. If there already are three or four conference areas, check to see how long students are conferring. If they are staying too long, set five-minute time limits so that others have an opportunity to use those areas.
4. If you notice a few restless students, invite them to join the group you are meeting with at the conference table so that they can receive feedback on their writing or help the other writers.
5. Conduct briefer conferences at the group conference table to allow more students to join the group.
6. Have students stop writing to review the following workshop guidelines. (1) "It's OK to give or receive quick help with writing at your desk, but if you need to really discuss your writing, go to a conference area with a classmate." (2) "Use a soft voice when discussing writing. The sound of your voice shouldn't travel more than the length of a 12-inch ruler."
7. If the classroom becomes noisy despite your guidelines and precautions. Get your students' attention and say, "Your talking has become so loud that we can't hear each other at the conference table. I'd like you to work silently for the next several minutes."

CHAPTER FOUR

Putting It All Together: Teaching Writing

Now it is the time to get down to the really serious business of introducing your students to the writing process through stories from their lives. Like many other writing teachers, I find that it is much easier to guide children through the process and help them improve the quality of their writing if they write about what they already know— rather than what they imagine.

If you are trying the writing process approach for the first time, I'd like to show you the teaching possibilities that are inherent in the introductory workshops. Because they are particularly important for getting students of all ages started, I will describe the first two workshops in detail. For the remaining four workshops, I will outline only my teaching goals and provide brief summaries of each workshop's activities. If you are a primary teacher, you probably will want to establish your own goals, which will place less emphasis on the revision process than I do. In fact, no part of this workshop outline is chiseled in stone; for example, although I've conducted similar introductory workshops in many classrooms, discussions and reference charts never turn out the same, nor do my drafts. The appendix provides examples of reference charts only to suggest possibilities—you will find that the charts you and your students create throughout several workshops will be much more meaningful than any ready-made ones.

WORKSHOP 1: CHOOSING A TOPIC

What Students Need to Know about the Process

1. It is important to select a topic that matters to the writer.
2. Notebooks, activity sheets, and projects for sharing personal interests are useful sources for writing ideas.
3. Talking about a topic helps a writer recall important details and events.
4. Conferences help writers make decisions.
5. Writers use the proofreading marks to add (∧) and to delete (⌒) words and lines.

What Students Need to Know About Good Writing

1. Good writing is meaningful. Ideas for writing often spring from powerful feelings.
2. Good writing depends on the recall of specific, concrete details.
3. Good writing has a limited and clearly defined focus.

What Students Need to Know about Writers

1. Writers reveal themselves and their lives.
2. Writing is hard work.

Materials

Individual writing folders, writing notebooks, "All About Me" folders, lined draft paper, pencils, transparencies and an overhead projector (if a projector is not available, use 18" x 24" lined chart paper), one black felt tip marker.

Reference Charts

1. HOW TO FIND A TOPIC (*See Figure 18 on page 98 for an example.*)
2. WHAT WRITERS DO (*See Figure 19 on page 99 for an example.*)

Description

I begin by modeling how to find a topic that matters—one that I really want to spend a lot of time and energy on. My students brainstorm a list of readily available sources for topics. Following one of their suggestions, I look through my "All About Me" folder and take out my WHAT'S ON YOUR MIND form. (*See Figure 3 on page 20.*) I "think aloud" about which events or people represented in the sketches I could write about. Then on an overhead transparency sheet (or chart paper), I write the heading "Possible Topics," the day's date, and three writing ideas, but I leave a good-sized space in between each topic for notes.

1. My trip to California
2. My dog Terrence
3. Losing David in the park

"Starting to write something is so hard for me," I might say. I explain that I feel better when I can at least put this much down on paper. I continue, "It's important to list more than one topic possibility because I can't tell at first which might make the best story. Then I need to talk about several ideas to find the one I can remember best and feel most strongly about."

I discuss each writing idea on my list. I've deliberately included a broad topic such as a trip, a favorite topic among children. Writing about a trip, however, often turns into an uninteresting list of places visited. To show them how I go about narrowing a too-big topic, I jot down all of the trip's aspects—the airplane flight, meeting old friends, going to Disneyland, and finally the minor earthquake I experienced. Then I conclude by saying, "I'll delete the words 'My Trip to California' because I really have four different topics here. Since the part that I have strongest feelings about is the earthquake, I think I'll focus on that."

Using the delete symbol, I cross out my original topic and insert "The Earthquake" with a caret. Then I tell the stories about my late dog Terrence, and the time I lost my six-year-old in a park. After responding to my students' questions with additional information, I write a few brief notes in the spaces below each writing idea and then explain, "These notes will help me remember some of the things I've told you."

I continue by saying, "I think I'll write about my dog Terrence. I remember all his adventures and the trouble he got my family into. I also remember how I resented the extra work he gave me when he was a puppy and how my feelings changed when he was old and sick. Talking to you really helped me realize that Terrence was very important in my life. Still, I'll save my 'Possible Topics' sheet because it will come in handy when I finish writing about Terrence."

As I distribute lined paper for listing "Possible Topics," I ask my students to look through their writing notebooks and their "All About Me" folders to find different subjects or topics they might want to write about. I also remind them that they may have to break a too-big topic into smaller parts as I did. "Look for whatever is most important to you," I urge, "and look for strong feelings, too, because they can help you remember."

As soon as two students complete their list of topics (some might have as many as four), I pair them up for topic conferences. Gradually other pairs join them. With so much talk going on at the same time, the classroom can get pretty noisy, so I send some conference partners to corners of the room and a few of the most responsible into the corridor. After several minutes of storytelling, most students know what they will write about. I advise those who haven't yet selected a topic, to think about their ideas

and choose one before our next workshop.

In a brief sharing session, I then have my students announce their writing topics, and we begin our first reference chart, WHAT WRITERS DO. I ask, "What did we do today?" Then using their words, I write something like the following on the chart.

1. In your notebooks and "All About Me" folders, look for three things you could write about. Write them down. If necessary, break up a big topic into smaller parts.
2. As you tell someone your stories, write down things you want to remember.
3. Pick the topic that means the most to you.

WORKSHOP 2: DRAFTING

What Students Need to Know about the Writing Process

1. Temporary titles help writers get started.
2. Writers draft freely without worrying about correct conventions.
3. Spaces left between lines of writing make drafts more legible and allow the writer to add or change words later on.
4. Writers develop their stories over time.
5. Writers collect ideas for future topics.

What Students Need to Know about Good Writing

1. Good writing demonstrates the writer's full knowledge of the subject.
2. Concrete details and specific information show the reader what is happening.

What Students Need to Know about Writers

1. Talk comes easier than writing.
2. Writers sometimes feel vulnerable when sharing their work.

Description

On the overhead screen, I show my following draft.

It is immediately obvious to my students that I have not included many of the details that I had talked about during my first

---

Draft #1

My Dog Terrence

When my family lived in California we got our first ~~dog~~ puppy. I really

didn't want a dog but my husband and children did.

I knew that I would have to clean up the dog's <u>messes</u> no matter

what they promised. I was so mad. "I'll walk him every day", my son,

David, said. "I'll feed him every day", my daughter, Beth, said. Do you think

they kept their ~~did what they~~ promises? No! I had got stuck with all the

work. Terrence—that's what we named him—used to get in

lots of trouble, too.

---

demonstration. I explain that I've underlined a word when I wasn't sure of its spelling, but I didn't use a dictionary at this point because it's more important to get my ideas down on paper as quickly as I can. I also point out that I skipped spaces when I wrote to make the draft easier to read and also to give me a place to add words later on.

"I've written 'My Dog Terrence' as my title," I explain, "but it's only temporary. Still, it will help me stick to my subject until I come up with a better title."

Before reading my draft aloud, I let my students know how I feel about sharing an unfinished piece and what kind of help I'm hoping to get. "This is just a beginning," I explain, "and I feel a little nervous about reading it to you, but your questions will help me remember more specific facts and details about Terrence."

At this point my students usually ask me about the kind of trouble Terrence got into.

With all the visual details and feelings I can recall, I respond to their questions by describing Terrence's fights with other dogs and his nightlong outings. "This discussion shows me how much easier talking is easier than writing," I emphasize. "I'll add some of the things I talked about, but, of course, my story won't be completed by our next workshop. It will take me a while to develop my story and make it as interesting as it can be."

After thanking my students for helping me remember more about my subject, I encourage them to decide on a temporary title and begin to write their own drafts. Then I point out the route I'll be taking as I move from desk to desk for brief one-to-one conferences. We also discuss what they might do if they get stuck before I reach them. The chart we begin to develop offers only two options today, but over time we will generate additional strategies for blocked writers.

What To Do When
You Are Stuck

1. Make a storyboard. Use stick figures to show the main scenes of your story. (See pg. 47)
2. Put your draft in your folder and write in your writing notebook. (*After my students write for about 20 to 30 minutes, we gather together for sharing time. To our WHAT WRITERS DO chart we add items 3 and 4, below.*)

~~~~~~

4. Write a temporary title and draft.

5. Talk more about your story.

~~~~~~

Then three or four volunteers read aloud their works-in-progress and respond to questions. Afterwards, I collect all of my students' writing folders in order to review them before the next workshop.

WORKSHOP 3: RESPONDING AND REVISING

What Students Need to Know about the Writing Process

1. Writers receive and provide response in group conferences.
2. Revision involves adding, deleting and moving parts around to make sense.
3. Drafts can be messy because writers cut, paste, staple, and rewrite.
4. Writers turn to the works of favorite authors to find examples of effective introductions and dialogue.

What Students Need to Know about Good Writing

1. Good introductions focus on the topic, fit the mood of the piece, and engage the reader.
2. Dialogue often enlivens stories. Dialogue may be conversation or inner thoughts.

What Students Need to Know about Writers

1. Writers need to set their own conference agendas.
2. Writers need positive and sensitive feedback.

Reference Charts and Forms

1. WHAT WRITERS DO
2. WHAT TO DO WHEN YOU ARE STUCK
3. HOW TO HELP A WRITER (*See Figure 21 on page 101.*)
4. SURVEY OF DAILY WRITING PLANS (*See Figure 27 on page 107.*)

SUMMARY

In my writing demonstration, I show my experiments with different introductions and dialogue. My students look through books they are reading to find and share effective examples of both. After telling me their writing plans for the day, some students write as others join group conferences. To the WHAT WRITERS DO chart, we add the following points.

~~~~~~

6. Write an interesting introduction.

7. Revise and change parts if necessary.

~~~~~~

WORKSHOP 4: IMPROVING WRITING

What Students Need to Know about the Writing Process

1. Writers devise their own strategies for inserting new information by using footnotes with matching symbols, numbers, colors, etc., inserted into the text.
2. All drafts, including unused pieces, are saved for future use or reference.

What Students Need to Know about Good Writing

1. Effective endings should tie things up and fit the mood of the piece.
2. Titles should grab a reader and relate to the story.
3. Good titles often can be taken from words in the story's text.

What Students Need to Know about Writers

1. Writers learn from each other's processes and writing experiments.
2. The changes writers make in drafts are evidence of their thinking and hard work throughout the process.

Reference Charts and Forms

1. WHAT WRITERS DO
2. SURVEY OF DAILY WRITING PLANS

SUMMARY

I show my students everything in my writing folder—my list of possible topics, strips of writing cut out of my piece, and notes to myself. "Nothing is thrown away," I explain, "because each bit of unused writing shows how much thinking and effort I put into developing my piece."

My demonstration also focuses on finding an ending and a title for my story about Terrence. I explain that I've seen endings such as "The End" or "Then I went home," but I wanted a more satisfying conclusion, one that would tie everything up. After

responding to my ideas for an ending, we discuss several titles I might use. Then, before my students write, I ask for and record their writing plans. During sharing time, they share their own revision strategies and to our WHAT WRITERS DO chart we add the following two points.

8. Work on a satisfying ending.

9. Try different titles.

The remaining What Writers Do points can be filled in when you teach the editing process (pg. 51):

10. Fill out an Am I Ready to Edit form (fig. 23, pg. 103). Have a conference.

11. Fill out an Editing Steps form (figs. 24 or 25, pgs. 104 or 105).

12. Give the edited draft to your teacher.

13. Illustrate a cover. Print the title and the author's name.

WORKSHOP 5: POLISHING WRITING

What Students Need to Know about the Writing Process

1. Editing is the final stage of revision. It follows the development and organization of meaningful ideas and events.

2. Editing begins by reading through a piece and making word changes that improve the writing.

3. A self-check system helps students know if they are ready to edit.

What Students Need to Know about Good Writing

1. An effective piece of writing is clear and concise.

2. Strong verbs and specific nouns help the reader see what is happening.

What Students Need to Know about Writers

A writer knows and cares about language.

Reference Charts and Forms

WHAT WRITERS DO

AM I READY TO EDIT? (*See Figure 23 on page 103.*)

SUMMARY

The form AM I READY TO EDIT? covers the criteria for good writing that I have worked on and discussed with my students thus far. Guided by this checklist, I "think aloud" about what I have done so far to improve my writing and conclude that I am satisfied. Then, demonstrating the first step in editing, I read aloud my writing to see if sentences and words make my meaning clear. If I am teaching students in grades three or higher, I replace weak verbs with verbs that show action (e.g. went/raced) and general nouns with specific ones (e.g. park/Springdale Park). I also delete unnecessary or over-used words.

WORKSHOP 6: PROOFREADING

What Students Need to Know about the Writing Process

1. The editing process involves self-editing, peer-editing, and teacher-editing.

2. In the final steps in editing, students proofread to correct spelling, punctuation, capitals, paragraphs, and grammar.

What Students Need to Know about Good Writing

Good writing reflects attention to proper form and the conventions of mechanics, spelling, syntax, and grammar.

What Students Need to Know about Writers

Editing is an on-going challenge and learning experience for all writers.

Reference Charts and Forms

WHAT WRITERS DO

SURVEY OF DAILY WRITING PLANS

EDITING STEPS (*See Figures 24 and 25 on pages 104–105.*)

POSSIBLE WAYS TO PUBLISH (*See Figure 26 on page 106.*)

SUMMARY

I begin this workshop by recording my students' writing plans for the day. The survey indicates just what I had expected—my students are at various stages of the writing process at this point in time.

Then while looking at one or two pages of my edited draft, students brainstorm a list of things to look for when editing (capitals, punctuation, spelling, paragraphs), and I copy them onto the chalkboard. In primary classrooms, the editing steps are simplified, of course.

Next I distribute and discuss the individual checklists EDITING STEPS for self-editing and peer-editing. Finally I show my students a box labeled "Editor-in-Chief" where the edited drafts should be placed for me to check. I explain that while a draft is in the Editor-in-Chief box, the writer can make and illustrate a cover, write a blurb about the author, and/or write a dedication. (This gives me time to edit at my leisure.) Within a few days, the writer and I will meet to discuss one or two of the most crucial editing problems in the draft.

Afterwards some children continue to develop their writing, and those who are ready to edit work together in pairs. Although the final form for my own work which appears on page 52 is the conventional essay, I encourage my students to consider a variety of different ways to publish their writing by showing them the list POSSIBLE WAYS TO PUBLISH. (*See Figure 26 on page 106.*)

EDITING FOR THE MECHANICS AND CONVENTIONS OF WRITING

As most teachers have learned from experience, the mechanics and conventions of writing need to be taught and retaught at every grade level when children need them and can understand their purposes. Past notions of sequential skills no longer apply for children who begin writing in the early years. Quotation marks, for example, once thought to be an advanced skill, can be learned by first graders who use dialogue. On the other hand, the use of end punctuation, although introduced in the primary grades, sometimes eludes even many upper elementary students.

Another interesting phenomenon that I've discovered is that overuse often follows the introduction of a new skill. Therefore, if you teach your students to use exclamation points, you can expect to see them everywhere for a while. If you teach about quotation marks, expect to see lots of dialogue.

SHARED EDITING

After obtaining the writer's permission, photocopy (or recopy) a draft with a specific writing problem—the absence of capital letters, for example— onto an overhead transparency. Then after reading the draft aloud, ask your students to hunt for all the words that require capital letters. After you write the capitals they identify on the transparency in a colored marker, ask them which rules they've already learned for using capitals and list them on a chart. Show examples of one or two uses they don't mention—such as the first letter of words in a title—and add these to the chart. You can use this strategy for teaching other writing conventions such as end punctuation, quotation marks, paragraphs, apostrophes, and commas.

REFERENCE CHARTS

During an editing conference with a student, copy a sentence that needs to be corrected onto a chart. Then using a colored marker, highlight and explain the correction. Finally ask the child to help you teach that lesson to the whole group. It's a good idea to encourage your students to always refer to these charts when they edit. Reference charts and shared editing are just two examples of editing mini-lessons you can use to teach a wide variety of writing conventions.

Final Draft

Terrence the Terror

I never wanted a dog. I had been raised in a city apartment where pets were not welcome, so I was annoyed when my husband and children brought home a wire-hair puppy one day. I knew that I would get stuck with all the chores and have to clean up the dog's messes no matter what they promised.

"I'll walk him every day," my son, David said.

"I'll feed him twice a day," my daughter, Beth said.

Do you think they kept those promises? NO! I had to do all the work. And what's worse, Terrence used to get into lots of trouble, too. As he got older, Terrence started to explore the neighborhood and even the nearby beach. He'd stay out all night and come home in the morning smelling of fish. Once he even came home smelling like a skunk. My husband had to give him a tomato juice bath to get rid of the smell.

When Terrence got older and bigger, he got into more trouble. For example, whenever a male dog came onto our lawn, Terrence would attack. Once he had his jaws around a dog's neck. I screamed, "Bad dog!" and tried to pull Terrence off the dog. I grabbed Terrence's collar and pulled hard, lifting him and the other dog up in the air. Finally Terrence let the little dog go. It wasn't hurt, but I had a backache for a week after all that pulling.

But there was another side to Terrence the Terror as I had begun to call him. He was a good friend to David and Beth—following them to the park, fielding their balls, and sleeping next to them as they watched tv at night.

When my husband was away, we always felt safe because Terrence barked fiercely at every sound. Then Terrence got old and sick and he died. It was then that I realized how my feelings toward him had changed over the years. I had come to love Terrence the Terror after all.

EDITING "LONG" PIECES

Self-editing and recopying can be an overwhelming task for young children and for older students who write lengthy texts.

One way to handle this problem is to have your students proofread in steps. For example, first they should attempt to correct end punctuation marks independently. Then they should confer with you or a particularly able peer just on another punctuation mark such as quotation marks. Next, they should correct any capitalization errors and follow this step with another conference, and so on.

If a story is too long for a youngster to edit and recopy, suggest that it be divided into two "chapters." Then the writer can edit and recopy only the first chapter, and the unedited section of the draft can be attached to the good copy of the first chapter. You also could give the student the option of working on the unedited section at a later time.

You probably will find that after a draft has been edited by three people—the student, a peer, and you—errors will still appear in the final copy. The truth is that there is no such thing as a perfect paper. Therefore, you can simply let the paper go "as is," or you may choose to correct the mistakes lightly in pencil and return the paper to the writer for further changes.

SPELLING

Simply correcting students' spelling errors does little to help them improve as spellers. You may want to try an approach adapted from Australian writing experts, Jo-Ann Parry and David Hornsby (*Write On: A Conference Approach*, Heinemann, 1988), that provides systematic attention and practice in spelling during the editing process. Most teachers who use this system say it works better than the weekly spelling lists in workbooks.

Give your students the TRY AGAIN! form to problem-solve their way through the misspelled words in their drafts. (*See Figure 7, which follows on page 54.*) First, copy the words exactly as the child spelled them. If you don't have time to do that, simply underline the misspelled words in the draft.

Of course, you should limit the words to the number you think each child can handle.

Tell the student to look at the "TRY AGAIN!" form or the underlined words in their drafts and try to spell the misspelled words correctly in the FIRST TRY column. If the first try doesn't result in a correct spelling, place a check above each letter in the child's spelling that belongs in the word. For example, if the child had spelled "ghost" as "gost" you would check each of those letters to let the student know how many letters he or she was able to identify even though the word is still incorrectly spelled. This strategy helps students to think about spellings and, at the same time, it allows them to feel good about themselves. Even poor spellers are amazed and gratified to discover that they know many letters in a word.

If after a second try, the word is still incorrect, write the standard spelling in the right hand column. Then on a LEARN TO SPELL IT! form, the student should practice the spellings you had to provide. (*See Figure 8, which follows on page 55.*) This process won't require as much of your time as you may think because it is accomplished in small "bites," and each step requires only a few minutes of input. Remember, as well, that all students will not reach this point of the editing process at the same time.

You may also want your students to copy the correct spellings above the misspelled words in their drafts. Working in pairs, they can periodically test each other on words that stumped them on their first two tries. Following are some other strategies to help your students hone spelling skills.

A Ring of Words

Provide each student with a ring of blank cards. These can be made by punching a hole in each card and putting them on a round binder ring or string. On separate cards, write the standard spelling of words that your students could not correctly spell when editing. After they study their words, have them work with a partner who should "test" them to see which words they can spell correctly. Then have them star or check the spelling words they've mastered.

FIGURE 7

Name: _____

TRY AGAIN!

DATE	COPY WORD	FIRST TRY	SECOND TRY	STANDARD SPELLING

FIGURE 8

LEARN TO SPELL IT!

Practice the words you need to know. Here's how:

1. Look at the word in the Standard Spelling column on your TRY AGAIN! sheet. Say it.

2. Cover the word and try to remember the letters in it.

3. Write the word in the first column on this sheet. (Don't peek!)

4. Check it.

5. Use the remaining columns and repeat steps 1–4 two more times.

A Personal Dictionary

Have your students record the words they could not self-correct when editing in an alphabetically indexed notebook. (A file box and index cards arranged alphabetically will work as well.) Then follow the same procedures for studying and "testing" described above.

Wall Charts

On a wall chart have your students write the commonly used words they just learned to spell on their TRY AGAIN! forms. They may also contribute words to charts that focus on spelling rules such as the following.

1. Words that end with silent <u>e</u>

2. Words that drop a silent <u>e</u> before adding *ing*

3. Words that need a doubled consonant before *ing* (swimming)

4. Words that end with the suffix <u>tion</u>

5. Words that sound alike but are spelled differently (their-they're)

PUBLISHING

After working hard at writing, your students should be allowed to experience the joy of sharing their work with others in the school community. Following is just a sampling of the many ways you can help them celebrate their writing.

STORYBOOKS

You will need two pieces of white or pastel oaktag for book covers, several single sheets of unlined paper for the pages, a stapler to staple the pages and covers together, 11/2" cloth tape for the spine that conceals the staples, and vinyl letters or labels with colored borders for the names of the title and author.

When the books are completed, student authors may wish to read them aloud to the class. After reading aloud, place them in the school library for other children to read, but not to borrow.

PUBLISHING AREAS

If bulletin boards aren't available, string wires for displaying writing on the walls of corridors. Ask your principal, school nurse, and librarian for space to display student writing on the walls of their offices and library.

A LITERARY MAGAZINE

Get parent volunteers to type your students' best pieces. Have your students design the covers, photocopy the pages, and assemble the anthologies. Together you should then brainstorm a list of people and places where the magazine should be sent or taken. For example, make prior arrangements with the school librarian to display a copy of the magazine in the library so that anyone in the library will be able to read the magazine.

READ-AROUNDS

Send notes to classroom teachers, the principal, librarian, school nurse, and other school personnel to let them know that a few students would like to come to their rooms to read their stories. List several five- or ten- minute time segments from which they may choose. Staple response forms to your students' stories for readers or listeners to fill out. Parents, friends, and relatives can also be readers. (*See Figure 9, which follows, and for a blank form, see Figure 29 on page 109 in the Appendix.*) Your students will enjoy reading comments about their work such as "Your story was so exciting!"

WRITING CONTESTS

Encourage your students to send their best work to the following publishers of children's writings. If possible, first obtain issues of the magazines so that you can show your students examples of winning entries.

Cricket League Story Contests
P. O. Box 300
Peru, Illinois 61354
(Writing must follow selected themes).

Highlights for Children
Our Own Pages
803 Church Street
Honesdale, PA 18431

FIGURE 9

Title _My Trip to Disney World_

Author _Sarah Beck_

(Our young authors love an audience—please share your child's story with friends and relatives. Encourage them to sign and write comments!)

Signatures	Comments
Ms O'Farrell	Your book makes me think of my favorite place to visit.
Jessica Conte	I whant to epcot too
	I Liked your Book
	I Like Jumping in pools too.
Michael S.	I Liked the way she told me all the things she did
David Kronig	It had good Illutrasion
Jessica Djilani	It was iksiding
Miss Mitchell	I loved your book— especially the fireworks!

Stone Soup
  Children's Art Foundation
  P. O. Box 83
  Santa Cruz, CA 95063
  (Ask for free Writer's Guidelines.)
The Children's Album
  EGW Publishing Co.
  Box 6086
  Concord, CA 94524
  (Ask for free writing tips.)

COMPUTERS AND WRITING

TELECOMMUNICATIONS

Using modems and programs such as Logo Express, your students can send their writing as "electronic mail" to other classes in your school district. They also can participate in writing projects involving schools across the country by using FrEdmail and National Geographic's Kidnet.

The computer's capacity for facilitating the revising and editing processes and for producing clean-looking print—ready to be published—makes it easy for students to publish with a professional pride. I can find only three disadvantages to using word processors in the writing workshop. However, despite these disadvantages, the computer is a boon to young writers.

✦ There are seldom enough computers in the classroom.

✦ Students need additional time to practice keyboarding skills.

✦ Teachers don't get to see all the changes that a writer makes during the composing process. Talking with children about the reasons for changes gives teachers a window into their thinking.

WRITING ACROSS THE CURRICULUM

Once you give your students time to plan, draft, confer, revise, and edit their content area reports in writing workshops, you will see better and more interesting writing than you did in the past. In addition, the following strategies should help promote good content area writing.

✦ Prior to writing, give your students the opportunity to immerse themselves in a topic by reading extensively (not just textbooks, but informational trade books, especially picture books), viewing videotapes and filmstrips, engaging in group discussions, and most important, of course, participating in first-hand learning experiences involving direct observation or simulation activities.

✦ Have students keep learning logs or on-going journals in which they record their observations and reactions to readings and activities.

✦ Encourage shorter reports (one-and-a-half to three pages, handwritten) on a limited, focused topic rather than lengthy pages on a broad subject.

✦ Offer options and choices in topics. I've noticed that children are more willing to spend time researching information and reworking their drafts when they are passionately interested in a subject.

✦ Show your students a variety of formats and models for publishing non-fiction writing, such as magazine articles, alphabet "fact" books, "If You Lived in the Time of…" books, "Question-and Answer" books, riddle books, cartoon stories, poems, and picture books. (See figure 26 on page 106).

✦ Invite your sudents to write personal narratives or stories about their process of learning. Students involved in a study of pond life might include their first thoughts as they observed a pond creature under a microscope, what they said to a friend about their observations, descriptions of any problems they had, where they searched for information, and what they learned.

✦ Help your students find real purposes and audiences for their writing, such as letters, flyers, and newsletters.

FIGURE 10

SUMMARY CHART: Teaching About Writing in Six Introductory Workshops

ABOUT THE PROCESS

ABOUT GOOD WRITING

DAY ONE

- ✦ Select a meaningful topic by using notebooks and activities developed for personal sharing;
- ✦ Talk about ideas to recall visual details;
- ✦ Use editing marks to add and delete words.

- ✦ Writing ideas come from meaningful memories;
- ✦ Good writing depends on writer's knowledge of a subject;
- ✦ Good writing has a limited, defined focus.

DAY TWO

- ✦ Use a temporary title;
- ✦ Don't worry about being correct in a first draft;
- ✦ Allow plenty of time to develop a topic;
- ✦ Collect idea for future topics .

- ✦ Good writing displays sufficient information;
- ✦ Visual details show what is happening.

DAY THREE

- ✦ Have a conference to improve the writing;
- ✦ If necessary, add, delete, or move parts to improve the writing. Drafts may look messy;
- ✦ Look at the works of published authors for examples of introductions and dialogue.

- ✦ An effective introduction relates to the topic, fits the mood of the piece, and engages the reader;
- ✦ Dialogue may enliven a story. Dialogue may be conversation or thoughts.

DAY FOUR

- ✦ Invent ways to insert new information into the text;
- ✦ Save all drafts and unused bits and pieces of writing;
- ✦ Try out different titles to find the best one.

- ✦ Effective endings tie up ideas or events. They fit the mood of the piece;
- ✦ Effective titles relate to the story and attract readers. A particular phrase in the text may be used as a title.

DAY FIVE

- ✦ Use a self-check system to find out whether the writing is ready to be edited.
- ✦ Edit a piece by rereading the text and making word changes. Editing is the final stage of revision;

- ✦ Writing should be clear and concise;
- ✦ Strong verbs and specific nouns help the reader see what is happening.

DAY SIX

- ✦ Have three people edit a completed draft—the writer, a classmate, and the teacher.
- ✦ Proofread to correct spelling, punctuation, capitals, and grammar;
- ✦ Consider a variety of forms for publishing a piece of writing.

- ✦ Good writing reflects attention to the proper form and the conventions of spelling, syntax, and grammar.

Questions Teachers Ask About Teaching Writing

Q I don't feel comfortable about sharing my writing with students. Is there anything else I can do to "teach" my students the process?

A Try some of the following strategies:
1. Talk about what you would do as if you were writing. For example, you might first describe how you would go about selecting a writing topic. Then pack your story with visual details and tell it to the children.
2. Use your students as "models." Keep your process and knowledge goals in mind during conferences. For example, when students write, show a few how to use editing marks, write temporary titles, or add visual details. Then ask these students to demonstrate their strategies to their classmates. Add to your WHAT WRITERS DO chart after a demonstration.
3. Invite adult writers or would-be writers of children's stories into the classroom. Parents, colleagues, school personnel, and members of the community are usually eager to test their work on young audiences. Be sure to ask them to describe their process of writing. For example, they might show a writing notebook or folder and examples of their revisions.

Q What do parents say when they don't see students' writing coming home until the end of the school year?

A Parents are supportive once they know that portfolios are kept in school to give you and their children a meaningful way to look at growth and change over time. They will appreciate the opportunity to hear your evaluation of their child's progress and examine his or her portfolio during the report conferences. In Chapter 6, you will find suggestions for developing writing portfolios and sharing them with parents.

Q Some students get upset if I won't tell them how a word is spelled while they are writing a draft. How do you help students postpone spelling needs until they are ready to edit?

A In a writing demonstration, I show students the words I've underlined in my own draft for correction at a later time. I also let them know that it's more important for me to get my ideas onto paper than to stop to correct those words.

When students ask me for spellings during the drafting stage, I praise them for knowing that a word may not be spelled correctly and assure them that I'll help them "fix-up" these words later. Of course, students always can refer to wall charts that display commonly used words at any time. (*See "Wall Charts" on pages 56.*)

Q What role do workbooks play in helping students learn about grammar and other writing conventions?

A Research reveals that children learn grammatical and mechanical skills best in a meaningful context rather than through isolated practice. Still, some teachers like to keep several copies of different workbooks on hand for individual or group mini-lessons when their students demonstrate a need for learning a particular skill.

CHAPTER FIVE

Mini-Lessons: Teaching about Good Writing

Perhaps "Planting Seeds" or "Encouraging Marvelous Things to Happen" would be a more appropriate title for this chapter because they both describe what writing teachers are doing in every writing workshop. This chapter will show you what your students can learn through indirect, informal experiences such as demonstrations and conferences, and it will also provide examples of mini-lessons that you can use to teach your whole class some important elements of good writing.

INFORMAL WRITING EXPERIENCES THAT TEACH

Consider what your students learn when you model your own writing, confer with them on their writing, or point out examples of wonderful writing in good literature. In all of these informal ways you are teaching—sowing ideas that will help your students think of writing in a new way. In fact, you will find that your students will also do some of the teaching and, as a result, will learn from each other when they share and discuss their writing in groups and with the whole class.

DEMONSTRATIONS

Your students need on-going demonstrations to develop their writing skills. If you refer to the Summary Chart of my teaching goals for introductory writing demonstrations, you will see that each demonstration teaches several writing mini-lessons. (*See Figure 10 on page 59.*) It is only through continuing follow-up demonstrations, writing conferences, and mini-lessons that your students will be able to understand these ideas and techniques and use them when they write and revise.

TEACHER-STUDENT CONFERENCES

While a demonstration is one of the best ways to begin helping your students understand what writers should think about, conferences are necessary to help them apply what they've learned to improve their own writing. Therefore, to support your student writers during conferences, you may want to use the following strategies.

- ✦ Read a piece of writing to diagnose its most immediate problem.
- ✦ Listen carefully to determine the direction the writer wants to take.
- ✦ React with appropriate comments, questions, and options that stretch the writer's thinking while allowing the writer to maintain control of the piece.

Responding with "appropriate" comments and questions to a first draft is not difficult if you respond naturally and spontaneously to something that arouses your curiosity or touches your heart. Any open-ended question such as—"I don't know much about camping. Can you tell me more about it?"—should elicit a response that teaches both you and the writer something new. It's important to encourage your students to tell you their stories because so often they don't realize how much they actually know until they hear themselves talking. Then, based on this new information, you should ask additional questions that will "nudge" them to think about basic writing elements and structures. (*See pages 40–41 for examples of such questions.*) For example, if one of your students needs to consider what the one main point of his or her paper is, you could have that student discuss several topics and then ask which idea or event is most important.

To see how this strategy of questioning might work in a conference, read both the following "bare-bones" draft written by a second grader and the transcription notes of the student's two-and-a-half-minute draft conference. The notes show how the teacher's questions not only helped the writer discover his one main point but also develop his ideas.

Draft #1

SKIING IN BROMLEY

I went skiing in Bromley with my father. It was fun. I only fell once. I was driving home from skiing we had two bumps. It was scary. After that I felt nervous.

THE CONFERENCE

Teacher: How's your story coming along, Eddie?

Eddie: I don't know. I think I'm finished. I don't know what else to write.

Teacher: Well, let's see. You know your title really makes me want to read this story. I don't know too much about skiing, but I'd like to learn more about it from you...Oh, I see you also tell about the car bumping on the drive home. So do you also want to tell about that?

Eddie: Yeah, because I was so scared.

Teacher: How come?

Eddie: The road was so icy and the car bumped.

Teacher: Were you hurt?

Eddie: No, but the car had a dent on the side, and my father was so mad.

Teacher: He was mad?

Eddie: Yeah, it was my grandfather's car. That's why.

Teacher: Did you dent the other car, too, when you bumped into it?

Eddie: We didn't bump a car. We drove into the bumper on the side of the road. Crack! I was sitting in the back and I jumped. I didn't know what was happening.

Teacher: Oh, I understand now. Well, Eddie, it sounds as though you have two stories you could write about here: skiing and the car accident. You did have a lot to say about the car trip. Which do you really want to write about first?

Eddie: The car trip because it was so scary. It was really scary.

Teacher: So what would you call it then?

Eddie: A Scary Car Trip

Teacher: You were really scared.

Eddie: Well, it happened again because there was so much ice.

Teacher: Oh, no!

Eddie: I was so scared. I was shivering.

Teacher: What a nightmare!

Eddie: I thought I'd have nightmares, but I didn't.

Teacher: Well, it sounds as though you picked a good title then! So what will you do now?

Eddie: I'm going to write a story about the scary car trip.

Following is Eddie's final story. It was completed after an editing conference. You'll notice that he has limited his topic to the car trip that he developed his story with much, but not all, of the information he brought up during the conference.

Draft #2

A SCARY CAR TRIP

When my father and I were driving home from Vermont, we bumped. The road was so icy that we drove right into the bumper on the side of the road. I heard a big bump. My father got out of the car. He saw a dent in the side of the car. He looked mad to me. It was my grandfather's car. That's why he was so mad.

After that I was shivering. The road was icy again. We slipped again! I was more frightened than ever. I thought I would have nightmares, but I didn't.

PEER GROUP CONFERENCES

I have often heard students attribute a title, an introduction, and even an ending to a conference they had with other students. Keep in mind, however, that peer teaching is strongly influenced by the way you conduct your own group discussions. The kinds of questions you pose, the elements of writing you highlight, even the language you use—all serve as models for peer discussions. (*For group conference guidelines, see pages 39–40 in Chapter 3.*)

Sometimes in a group conference, your students will remember a particularly effective part or passage written by a classmate weeks or even months before. As a result, they will be able to draw on that memory to improve their own writing. The anecdote from a sixth grade classroom, which follows, illustrates the power inherent in peer teaching and learning.

Miss Little's students had listened carefully to Sadi's piece about a soccer game which ended, "So I tied the game up with forty-three seconds left in the game. I tried hard not to smile a lot because everybody would think I was showing off. But it was hard not to smile because I was so happy." Sadi then explained that his earlier drafts had not had that honest ending. They had just stated, "I was glad I helped my team win."

Afterwards in a discussion, the students agreed that the second ending was better because it was more lifelike. Miss Little emphasized that the second ending showed a real person in a real situation, and this kind of writing exhibits the special quality of "voice." Months later a student who had participated in that group conference wrote this comment about his own best piece of writing: "I kept thinking of Sadi's ending on his soccer game story so I revised my ending five times until I got mine to say exactly what I felt."

MINI-LESSONS

You will find that you can use mini-lessons to focus on any aspect of your writing workshop. In fact, early in the year you should even plan mini-lessons to discuss the use and care of new writing tools and materials as well as areas for conferences and sharing time. In other mini-lessons, you may want to share examples of writing by both published authors and student writers or have your students try out a new writing technique that you have demonstrated. You will find that the best ideas for mini-lessons actually grow out of the needs you perceive as you observe your students talking and writing.

OPPORTUNITIES FOR MINI-LESSONS

The mini-lessons outlined in the remainder of this chapter focus only on some of the elements of good writing. There are, of course, many reasons for other mini-lessons, including the following.

✦ To show students the location and use of materials you have collected for your writing workshop.

✦ To provide directions for making projects and crafts for personal sharing activities.

✦ To read aloud and discuss the works of published authors.

✦ To demonstrate ways to use writing notebooks.

✦ To develop and discuss reference charts, writing checklists, and editing forms.

✦ To demonstrate the use of a thesaurus, dictionary, and/or other writing and spelling aids.

✦ To discuss and establish conference and sharing guidelines.

✦ To demonstrate how to write for different purposes and different genres.

✦ To brainstorm criteria for evaluating

writing. (*See page 80 in Chapter 6.*)

✦ To brainstorm the contents of your students' Showcase Portfolios. (*See page 90 in Chapter 6.*)

TIPS FOR PREPARING MINI-LESSONS

1. Keep your mini-lessons brief by focusing on a single issue or concept. Five to ten minutes should be sufficient for a mini-lesson. Although an occasional mini-lesson will last more than ten minutes, it's important to reserve the major portion of your workshop time as writing time for your students.

2. Involve your students in some kind of activity during a mini-lesson—such as brainstorming, discussing, or writing. During such an activity, you can let them work in pairs, in small groups, or by themselves.

3. If you want your students to practice a new technique or skill—for example, replacing general words with more specific ones—limit the amount of practice you give them so that you will have time to let them share what they've written with the whole class or in small groups. Then, if several of your students haven't mastered the particular technique or skill, provide additional examples for them to practice on another day.

4. Keep multiple folders for your mini-lesson ideas. For example, you may want to keep a separate folder for each of the various elements of good writing—such as effective beginnings, vivid descriptions, and interesting endings. Many teachers also collect examples of play scripts, business and friendly letters, informational articles, newsletters, brochures, how-to pamphlets, and other real life models for their students to use during writing and publishing. Be sure also to save one folder for comments on writing made by your students' favorite authors.

5. Collect examples of good writing to use as models in your mini-lessons by

photocopying pages in books and by cutting out articles from magazines and newspapers. If you come across an idea for a mini-lesson in a professional book, in a workshop, or during a conversation with a colleague, jot it down on an index card and place it in the appropriate folder. You may need to obtain permissions from publishers before using photocopied material. When in doubt, don't photocopy, just jot down the idea in your own words.

MINI-LESSONS ON THE ELEMENTS OF GOOD WRITING

A lot of teaching about good writing goes on during demonstrations and conferences, but there are times when you will want to emphasize an important concept or technique by presenting it to your whole class and then by involving your students in a discussion or practice session. The mini-lessons in this section will focus on the following elements of good writing.

1. **Meaning**
   Good writing grows out of experiences and ideas that the writer knows and cares about.

2. **Clarity and Development**
   Good writing uses sufficient information and concrete, visual details.

3. **Organization**
   Good writing has a limited, defined focus and is organized logically with an effective beginning and a satisfying ending.

4. **Clear, Precise Language**
   Good writing is concise and contains few unnecessary words and repetitions. Strong verbs and specific nouns clearly show the reader what is happening.

5. **Conventions**
   Good writing exhibits appropriate usage, spelling, and the mechanics of punctuation, capitalization, and indentation of paragraphs.

MEANING MINI-LESSON

When I ask my students what the hardest part of writing is for them, many respond, "Finding something to write about." One way to help your students find a meaningful topic is by sharing writing samples of students' personal experiences that reflect strong feelings. After reading one or two pieces aloud, ask your students how they think the writers got their ideas. For example, you could ask questions such as the following.

✦ Why do you think the writer remembered so much about the time she got a shot in the doctor's office?

✦ Why do you think Peter wrote about missing the Thanksgiving play?

✦ What made these experiences important to these writers?

Although their responses will vary, your students should recognize the strong feelings of each of these writers. Then explain how feelings—such as delight, fear, and anger—help writers recall important times in their lives. If you do not have your own samples, you may want to use one of the following.

"Getting a Shot"
by Lu-San (*grade 2*)

Once I had to have a shot. I was afraid. My father said, "It will be all right." I wasn't sure. Then he said, "The needle isn't big."

I was bored in the car. I seemed to be falling asleep. When I woke up, I found myself in a room. There were bottles. There were also medicines.

I could see a woman. I didn't know she had a needle in her hand. When I could see the needle, I didn't want to get the shot. But it happened so quickly, I couldn't convince my father it would hurt.

The shot hurt! I said, "Ouch." I was glad the shot was over.

"Where Are the Strawberries?"
by Lawrence (*grade 3*)

The first time I picked strawberries I was in Florida. This is how I would pick a strawberry. I would pick a strawberry and hop. I was hopping because I was happy. Then I would ask my grandmother if I was doing fine and she would say, "You picked all the green ones." Well, I was only four years old.

After that I would pick fresh, red berries. I couldn't wait until that night when I would have strawberries and cream.

"No Thanksgiving Play for Me"
by Danny (*grade 6*)

"Can I go to school tomorrow?" I asked my mom. "My cough is almost gone."

"We'll see," she said. But by the way she said it, it sounded like no.

The next morning I woke up to see kids walking to school. I knew there would be no Thanksgiving play for me. As the day dragged by I wanted to call Christine to see if it had gone well.

"I can call Christine now!" I thought. "It's 3:30. She has to be home."

But what she told me made me not glad. It had gone well.

"It was terrific," she told me.

That made me angry. I wasn't supposed to go well without me. By the end of the phone call I felt like crying. I hated my class for doing well. I hated my mom for not letting me go. Most of all I hated Kate for getting my favorite line and solo.

Of course, I've calmed down a lot since fifth grade, but whenever I look back on that day I always think, "Why did it have to be me?"

Additional Ideas

Use the writing samples shown above or your own samples for a series of mini-lessons to discuss specific details, dialogue, titles, beginnings, endings, and voice.

CLARITY MINI-LESSON

One of the most common problems young writers face is transferring the image they have in their minds into words that will transmit a similar image to their readers' minds. To help your students notice and record visual details, distribute copies of the following excerpts (or similar ones) and say,

"These excerpts come from the writing of well-known authors. Let's see what they can teach us about good writing. Imagine that you've turned on a television set in your mind. While I read to you, listen for words that put pictures on the screen." After reading the excerpts, give your students copies of them and suggest that they work with a partner to identify and discuss the words and phrases that helped them mentally see a picture. Then ask them to draw an illustration of their favorite excerpt.

Iggie's House
by Judy Blume

"She studied her mother, standing like a statue in the doorway. Mom was wearing her work clothes—an old blue denim skirt and a faded striped shirt with the sleeves rolled up. Her face was smudged with dirt."

Paddington at Large
by Michael Bond

Paddington loves to eat and he gets hungry just looking at picture of food. For example, his stomach starts to growl when he looks a picture on the cover of a magazine that shows "a golden brown roast chicken resting on a plate laden with bright green peas, bread sauce, and roast potatoes. Alongside the chicken there was a huge sundae oozing layer upon layer of fruit and ice cream."

Tales of a Fourth Grade Nothing
by Judy Blume

Sheila, Jimmy, and Peter are working together on a project for school. In the following excerpt, one child describes the materials they will use.

"We keep our equipment under my bed in a shoe box. We have a set of Magic Markers, Elmer's glue, scotch tape, a really sharp pair of scissors and a container of silver sparkle."

Additional Ideas

Using their favorite books, have your students find and share examples of writing that include concrete, visual details.

DEVELOPMENT MINI-LESSON 1

In real life you get to know people by the things they do and say (DIALOGUE AND ACTIONS). To illustrate this concept for your students, write this sentence on the chalkboard: "The mean teacher was angry." Then announce that you are going to act like a mean teacher. Begin, for example, by rapping on a desk with a ruler and shouting something like, "One more sound and everyone stays in for recess." If your students laugh at this point, scowl and fold your arms across your chest and say "I heard someone laugh." Turn abruptly then and write on the chalkboard, "Today's homework—25 multiplication problems."

Then—as yourself—turn to your students and ask them to describe your previous words and actions. As they do, write their statements on the chalkboard. Finally, encourage them to compare this detailed description to the original sentence "The mean teacher was angry." Your students should easily conclude that a character's actions and words show, rather than tell, what a person is really like.

Additional Ideas

Read aloud excerpts from popular works of literature to demonstrate how professional writers reveal characters' temperament or feelings through their words and actions. As you read the excerpts, have your students jot down examples and then discuss them afterwards. You might want to use the following sources or ones of your own.

1. *Miss Nelson is Missing* shows the actions of a "mean" teacher. Read Harry Allard's description of Miss Viola Swamp as she introduces herself to the class. Your students will enjoy comparing Harry Allard's portrayal of Miss Swamp to their own descriptions of your actions in the previous lesson.

   "A woman in an ugly black dress stood before them. 'I am your new teacher, Miss Viola Swamp.' And she rapped the desk with her ruler. 'Where is Miss Nelson?' asked the kids. 'Never mind that!'

   snapped Miss Swamp. 'Open those arithmetic books!' Miss Nelson's kids did as they were told."

1. In *Ramona the Brave,* Six-year-old Ramona and her classmates have made paper bag owls. Susan copies Ramona's owl down to the smallest detail. Then their teacher selects Susan's owl for display rather than Ramona's. Beverly Cleary shows the reader the actions of an angry child.

   "Ramona stuffed her crayons into the box so hard that she broke several, but she did not care...Now everyone would think Ramona had copied Susan's owl instead of the other way around...With both hands she crushed her owl, her beautiful wise owl, into a wad and squashed it down as hard as she could. Then, with her head held high, she marched to the front of the room and flung it into the wastebasket."

ORGANIZATION MINI-LESSON 1

If you teach writing, you have probably seen many narratives that lose their impact because they lack a focus or main point (UNIFYING IDEA). Sometimes a subject is too broad because the writers want to tell everything they know about it—such as a trip they've taken or all about horses. Young writers also may wander off a topic by including irrelevant information—"and then we had lunch and played basketball"—when writing about the damage caused by a flood. The following activity will help your students limit their own topics and give them conference strategies for helping each other.

Read aloud or distribute copies of a draft that needs a unifying focus such as the following one, which was written by a third grade student:

For my birthday my friends and I watched Snow White on tv. We had pizza and cake and soda. For one present I got a bald Cabbage Patch Kid. After my party I went to my grandmother's house to play with my cousins. I brought a few toys there. My cousin's name is Linda. We played with each other. When I got home I played with all my toys. Then I played with my brother. It was a fun day.

Then explain the background of the writing of this draft by saying that Liza, in wanting to write about her birthday, told about everything she did that day that was fun. Later during a peer conference, Liza's friend Todd asked several questions that helped her see that she really had several different stories in this one piece. Realizing that she had no unifying idea, Liza then revised her draft. As your students listen to Liza's final draft, ask them to try to determine what questions Todd might have asked and what Liza's responses might have been.

HOW HECTOR TURNED INTO VICTORIA

For my birthday I got a present. It was a bald Cabbage Patch Kid called Hector Reed. It was a boy but I changed it into a girl. Here is how I did it. I put a dress on her that I took it off another doll I had. Then I put my red ribbon around her head and my chain necklace around her neck. I pasted sparkles on her ears to look like earrings. Now her name is Victoria Rina and she has blue eyes and she's still bald.

After your students compare the two drafts, discuss what made the second draft more interesting than the first (The first draft sounded like a list of things she did. The second draft had lots of details about the doll.) Then say something such as, "The one thing Todd did not do is to tell Liza what to write about because writers must make their own decisions." Then discuss questions—such as the following—that he might have asked her.

✦ What was the one best thing that happened that day?

✦ You tell about so many different things. Pick one part and tell me more about it.

✦ Tell me more about the part that was really special to you?

Additional Ideas

After providing examples of unfocused and focused drafts written by your own students, tell pairs of students to compare the two drafts. Ask them to take the parts of the writer and conferencer and role play a conference.

ORGANIZATION MINI-LESSON 2

The most important part of any piece of writing is its beginning or lead. Its job is to get readers' attention. Of course, the introduction must also relate to the topic. Your students should understand, however, that writers generally do not come up with good introductions (otherwise known as effective leads) as soon as they begin to write. A good beginning usually is the result of brainstorming, experimentation, and/or response from other writers. After you project the following beginnings on an overhead screen or distribute copies of them, tell your students that writers use different techniques to grab attention. Then ask them to decide which of the two beginnings in each set they prefer and explain their choices.

If you teach middle or upper elementary students, encourage them to look for specific techniques (action, dialogue, question, interesting fact) the writers used to attract a reader.

"Poor Kitty" (*grade 4*)
Lead 1. Yesterday I was walking with my cat Kitty and a car nearly hit her.
Lead 2. The car screeched to a stop: Eeeeek! It had almost run over Kitty.

"A Halloween I'll Never Forget" (*grade 5*)

Lead 1. On Halloween night I went to Liz Wood's slumber party.
Lead 2. It was a pitch-black, windy night when I arrived at Liz Wood's house for a slumber party.

"Shamoo" (*grade 3*)
Lead 1. When I was in Florida my family and I went to Sea World.
Lead 2. Shamoo is a fourteen and a half foot long killer whale. He is trained to talk.

"An Interview with Mike Madison" (grade 6)

Lead 1. Mike likes to play soccer. Mike remembers how he made a goal in a soccer game four years ago.

Lead 2. "I better make this shot or my team will lose for sure. My foot feels like a lead weight," thought twelve year old Mike Madison.

Additional Ideas

Use experiments with different beginnings written by your own students for class discussion. You also could encourage your students to share and discuss introductions of the books they are reading.

CLEAR, PRECISE LANGUAGE MINI-LESSON 1

One way to help your students become aware of the beauty of clear and succinct language is to immerse them in poetry. Poets must search for the clearest way to say precisely what they mean. Of course, picking apart a poem to identify its words and phrases will quickly squash the joy of poetry. As a result, you may want to engage your students in the more pleasurable activity of pantomiming or moving to the language of poetry. However, not just any poems will do. You'll need to select specific poems that suggest movement or use any the following poems for this activity. The poem "The Base Stealer," for example, uses precise words to inspire actions such as "fingertips pointing the opposites," "bouncing tiptoe like a dropped ball," and "running a scattering of steps sidewise."

"The Base Stealer"

by Robert Francis

Poised between going on and back, pulled
Both ways taut like a tightrope-walker,
Fingertips pointing the opposites,
Now bouncing tiptoe like a dropped ball
Or a kid skipping rope, come on, come on,
Running a scattering of steps sidewise,
How he teeters, skitters, tingles, teases,
Taunts them, hovers like an ecstatic bird,
He's only flirting, crowd him, crowd him,

Delicate, delicate, delicate, delicate—now!

If you teach young children, you may want to read a poem aloud—perhaps more than once—for them to enjoy. Then divide the class into groups to act it out. You could even show the poem on a chart or overhead projector and suggest that different groups use its words and phrases to help them plan their movements.

Older students, however, should work in groups, each using copies of a different poem to read and act out for the class. Let each group determine who will read the poem aloud and who will do the movements. Ask your students to read the poem to themselves first and then discuss it with their group. Encourage them to point out lines they like or ask questions about parts that they don't understand. After they have read and talked about the poem, tell them to highlight or underline the words in the poem that will help them plan their movements. (You may need to allow more time for this activity than the usual ten minutes, or you can spread the group pantomime performances over several days.)

After your students have performed their pantomimes, you may want to ask them to write their favorite words and lines in their writing notebooks or onto posters along with some illustrations. In later writing conferences with your students, help them recall the language they learned through this activity as they revise their own writing.

Additional Ideas

Have your students read and discuss samples of clear, precise writing that is written by both students and professional authors.

A second idea is to ask your students to copy examples of language that inspires movement from their own writing onto oaktag or sturdy strips of paper. Display the strips on a bulletin board with the heading "Writing with Power." A third idea is to have your upper elementary students read sports articles. As they read, tell them to look for and record verbs that suggest action images—such as *bumped, fumbled, bounced, fouled, rebounded, grabbed,* and *dunked.* Then suggest that they refer to these lists when they write sports stories or any other action story.

CLEAR, PRECISE LANGUAGE MINI-LESSON 2

"Be specific" is the advice you hear most often from professional writers. They suggest, for example, that if you replace general words—such as *fruit*—with *apple* or *Rome apple*, your readers will be able to visualize a familiar image and sometimes will even be able to "taste" or "smell" the apple. To help your students understand the importance of using specifics, write the following sentence on the chalkboard.

Eddie went to the store and bought his lunch.

Then ask your students to name a verb that shows how Eddie might have gone to the store (*ran, bicycled, jogged, walked*). Take this opportunity to model the use of proofreading marks as you delete *went* and insert one of their suggestions with a caret.

Then ask for the name of a neighborhood food store to replace the general word *store*. Finally, have your students name specific kinds of foods to replace the word *lunch*. Your revised sentence might look something like this:

Eddie jogged to the Heathcote Deli to buy a salami and cheese sandwich and a container of chocolate milk.

To start a discussion that compares the revised sentence with the original one, say something such as, "If you were asked to illustrate the scenes described by these sentences, which sentence would you prefer to use? What pictures would you draw? Which words put those pictures in your mind? What do specifics do for a reader?"

Additional Ideas

Ask your students to reread their own writing to look for general words that could be replaced by more specific ones. Also have them share examples of the specific words that they have used. A thesaurus or dictionary may be helpful for finding colorful synonyms.

CLEAR, PRECISE LANGUAGE MINI-LESSON 3

Since the concept of specific words is so important, you may want to give your students additional practice with this technique. Provide your students with a list of general words such as a car, a noise, vegetable, said, nice, a dog, flowers, money, a game, and a desert. Have them work in pairs to generate specific words to replace the general words.

CLEAR, PRECISE LANGUAGE MINI-LESSON 4

Traditionally, sentence combining exercises have always been postponed until high school, but I've discovered that students can learn this important technique for writing more interesting, natural sounding sentences as early as third or fourth grade. To teach sentence combining, write the following short sentences on the chalkboard.

I went ice skating. I went on Saturday.

Ask your students how they could say the same thing in one sentence instead of two. They may suggest "I went ice skating on Saturday." or "On Saturday I went ice skating." If they have difficulty seeing these connections, suggest they look for any repeated words that could be deleted in the following sentences.

I had a birthday party. We ate pizza. We ate cake. (We ate pizza and cake at my birthday party. Or, At my birthday party we ate pizza and cake.)

Additional Ideas

Pair up your students and as they read their partner's writing, have them look for short sentences that could be combined. Remind them, however, that not all short sentences need to be combined; there are times when short sentences add a punch to writing or show fast paced action—such as the following excerpt from a students' story about a soccer game.

"Pass, Dave, pass!" I cried. David looked up. He saw me and passed. I slid. My right foot met the ball. I scored!"

CLEAR, PRECISE LANGUAGE MINI-LESSON 5

When your students have learned to combine two or more ideas into a single sentence, they may run into a new problem—word clutter. For example, a combination of these short sentences "I was playing soccer. I was playing soccer with Pete. Pete is my best friend." may produce "I was playing soccer with Pete who is my best friend." Although this sentence is a great improvement over the three short sentences, it can be strengthened even more by deleting the words *who is*.

> I was playing soccer with my best friend Pete.

Tell your students that good writers use fewer words to say the same thing in a simpler way. To help them learn how to do this, read aloud the paragraph shown on the following activity sheet so they can hear how it sounds before and after revision. Then after they identify the unnecessary words, have them practice deleting these words from the sentences.

Additional Ideas
After your students work in pairs to find unnecessary words in their own and in their partner's writing, have them delete the words using proofreading marks.

CLEAR, PRECISE LANGUAGE MINI-LESSON 6

Have you noticed how often writing growth and writing problems seem to go hand in hand? For example, as soon as young children learn to write a sequence of events to tell a complete story, many repeatedly use the word *and* to link one event or action to the next. Although this particular problem usually disappears in the upper elementary grades, older students simply overuse other words—such as *then*, *so* and *but*—when they write. To help your students find alternative ways to deal with repetitions, have them delete or replace the word *then* in the paragraph on page 73.

Additional Ideas
If repetitions of the words *and*, *so* and *but* seem to be a problem for your students, you may want to adapt the activity sheet shown on page 73 by writing the overused word you've selected in place of the word *then*. (You can use the student writing sample I've provided or one of your own.)

CONVENTIONS MINI-LESSON

Someone once said that **run-on sentences** are like sin—impossible to stamp out. The truth is that teachers at every grade level try to help their students eliminate this persistent problem because in school and in the real world run-on sentences interfere with communication. You can use the following activity sheet for several lessons on run-on sentences. All your students will need is a fresh run-on sentence to correct each time.

TEACHER-DESIGNED ACTIVITY SHEETS

The following suggestions show you how you can create your own activity sheets for covering any writing convention—such as the use of capital letters, verb tense agreement, or punctuation marks.

✦ Look at copies of several commercially published language arts skills books to see how they define the conventions

The following activity sheets provide practice in conventions regarding clarity, precise language, run-on sentences, and capitalization. To use the worksheets, make one copy for yourself, then white-out the answers in parenthesis before photocopying for the class.

CLIP THE CLUTTER!

1. Read the following paragraph to see how one student deleted unnecessary words that cluttered up his sentences.

John, ~~who is~~ my little brother, is a big pain. ~~The reason is~~ he always bothers me when I play football with my friends. I think that a seven year old is too young to play with ten-year-olds. This ~~is~~ a problem ~~which is~~ annoying.

2. Write the deleted words and phrases on the following lines.

(who is) _____   (the reason is) _____

(is a) _____   (which) _____

3. Delete unnecessary words from the following sentences. Then rewrite each sentence on the line below it. Notice that there may be several ways to rewrite a sentence. (Possible answers are given in parenthesis.)

✦ The reason I am late is because my alarm didn't ring.

_(I am late because my alarm didn't ring.)_____

✦ Lisa, who is my best friend, will go to camp with me.

_(Lisa, my best friend, will go to camp with me.)_____

✦ I like to go on rides that are exciting.

_(I like to go on exciting rides.)_____

✦ Checkers is a game which is simple.

_(Checkers is a simple game.)_____

TOO MANY THEN'S!

1. Read the following excerpt from Emily's story about how she changed from a girl into a horse.

Then I entered the den. My fifteen year old brother just stared at me. I didn't care. I sat down and started to watch the Bill Cosby show. Then my brother ran to my mother and said, "There's a horse in the house!"

Then, poof, I was myself again. Then my brother came back with my mother and she said, "Don't you dare call Emily a horse!"

Then my brother kept saying, "But, but, but..." for the rest of the night.

2. Notice that Emily used the word "then" too many times. There are two ways to eliminate this problem.

   a. Delete some then's.

   Example: ~~Then~~ she came into the room.

   b. Replace some then's with different words—such as afterwards, finally, suddenly, a few minutes later, meanwhile, and at last.

   Example: A few minutes later she came into the room.

3. On the following lines, write additional words that could be substituted for then. (Possible answers are given in parenthesis.)

   _____(next)_____   _____(later on)_____   _____(after that)_____

4. Revise the excerpt from Emily's story to eliminate or replace some of her

   repeated words. Use this mark (⌒) to delete a word, and use a

   caret (∧) to insert words.

FIX-UP THE RUN-ON

A run-on sentence occurs when two simple sentences are joined without any punctuation or a connecting word.

Example: Snails are unusual creatures they carry their houses on their backs.

Ways to Correct a Run-on Sentence.

1. Add punctuation. Change a lower case letter to a capital letter.

Example: Snails are unusual creatures. They carry their houses on their backs.

2. Add a connecting word—such as and, but, so, which, when, while, because, or before.

Example: Snails are unusual creatures because they carry their houses on their backs.

3. Change words around.

Example: Because they carry their houses on their backs, snails are unusual creatures.

Think about the three ways you might correct the following run-on sentence. Then write the corrected sentences on the lines below. (Possible answers are given in parenthesis.)

I saw so many sticks, rocks, and patches of grass I wondered how to ski around them.

1. Add punctuation.

(I saw so many sticks, rocks, and patches of grass. I wondered how to ski around them.)

2. Add a connecting word.

(When I saw so many sticks, rocks, and patches of grass, I wondered how to ski around them.)

3. Change words around.

(I wondered how to ski around so many sticks, rocks, and patches of grass.)

BE A CAPITALIZATION EXPERT!

Read the following rules for capitalizing words and study the examples.

1. Use a capital letter for the word "I".
Mother and I will help you.   I'll see you later.

2. Begin the first word of every sentence with a capital letter.
When will I see you again?   She wanted a puppy for her birthday.

3. Use a capital letter to begin names.

a person: Jane	a street: Popham Road
a holiday: Thanksgiving	a country or state: England; Ohio
a pet: my cat, Whiskers	a country's people: English
days of the week: Monday	a special group: Girl Scouts
months: March	a special place: Disneyland

4. Use a capital letter to begin the first word and the important words in titles. Notice that these titles are also underlined.
Books: <u>Charlie and the Chocolate Factory</u>

Magazines: <u>National Geographic</u>

Movies: <u>Home Alone II</u>

5. Use a capital letter to begin a sentence that needs quotation marks around it.
"This is the best day of my life!" James exclaimed.

6. Use a capital letter to begin the first word in the greeting and the closing of a letter.

Greeting	Closing
Dear Aunt Jane,	Sincerely,

7. Use a capital letter to begin an honorary title.
Dr. Smith   Mr. Fisher   Ms. Peters   Miss Nelson

Now use the rules you have just read to help you correct the errors in the following excerpt. Use the proofreading mark of three small lines under a letter for making a lower case letter a capital letter. (Example: henry)

My family and i were going to washington, D. C. for thanksgiving weekend. It started to drizzle. "it's raining, it's pouring, the old man is snoring," my brother sang happily. We stayed at the holiday inn in Alexandria, virginia from wednesday to sunday.

Questions Teachers Ask
About Mini-Lessons

Q Do I correct the practice forms my children complete during mini-lessons, and who keeps the forms?

A If you limit the amount of written practice your students have to do, they should have enough time to discuss and change their responses. Although students seem to learn more when they correct their own work, it's a good idea to collect the activity forms so that you can see how well each one understood the concept or skill. You also may want to have a small group conference with only those students who need more practice. If you have your students keep their activity forms in a separate folder or section of a looseleaf notebook, they can easily refer to them when revising or editing their writing.

Q Can some of the mini-lessons you suggest be used as homework assignments?

A They can, but then you will never know whether the student was able to complete the assigned task independently or received assistance from a parent. However, some activities such as "Fix-up the Run-on" can be repeated for homework with a different example of student writing.

Q Can I use the writing skill activities in my language arts workbooks for mini-lessons?

A Yes, but you will need to be selective. Look through a workbook, for example, to find challenging skills almost every student

needs to learn—such as the correct form for letter writing or how to punctuate dialogue. Be sure to choose worksheets that provide a clear example of the correct use of a skill and have a limited number of sentences for children to rewrite. These standardized sheets, of course, work best when you follow-up with a classroom demonstration and discussion.

Q How important is it to prepare a mini-lesson for every writing workshop?

A You don't need to prepare a mini-lessons for every workshop because there are countless opportunities for teaching and learning in your workshops. In fact, your students will be learning something important from you and from each other in every writing conference and in your whole class sharing time. Also think about how much children learn about good writing when you read aloud a book that they are able to then discuss.

CHAPTER SIX

Assessing and Evaluating Writing

Just as the teaching of writing has changed dramatically in recent years, so has the process of assessing and evaluating writing. In the past, before I taught writing as a process, evaluation seemed easy. I used a checklist of familiar writing conventions—such as "writes complete sentences" and "uses correct punctuation, capitals, spellings, and grammar." Following this list, I would write the terms *content* and *organization* to encompass all of the other nebulous qualities that made writing "good." I do believe that I could tell good writing apart from poor writing, but to tell the truth, I never articulated these criteria to myself, to my students, or to their parents.

Today my process of evaluation, like the writing process itself, is more complex. It both mirrors and determines the direction of my teaching, and it is based on on-going assessments—the continuous gathering and recording of students' daily work and other evidences of their learning and changes in their writing. However, I am no longer the sole evaluator. After my students collect evidence of their learning, they also evaluate their own work based on clearly articulated criteria.

This chapter will provide you with concrete information about assessment tools (the gathering of evidence) and it will describe evaluation processes (the ways that data may interpreted.) There are, of course, no recipes. The tools and procedures that you will learn about in this chapter reflect strategies that I have found effective and manageable in a variety of classrooms, but your goals, your students, and your classroom situation will be different than mine. Therefore, to make evaluation work in your classroom, you will need to develop questions for interviews, criteria for surveys, and strategies for portfolios that best meet your own needs. The best place to begin is by selecting only a few new tools and procedures, keeping in mind that every type of assessment has its unique advantages. Each will give you a different lens to look at the big picture of your students' learning.

CUMULATIVE WRITING FOLDERS

Cumulative writing folders contain the writing pieces—along with their drafts—that students develop and complete in their writing workshops during the school year. However, worksheets, homework assignments, and incomplete drafts usually are not included. Any kind of expandable folder that can accommodate a one-and-a-half- to two-inch collection of papers will serve as a cumulative folder. In fact, your students could easily create folders that are not only functional but also attractive.

Because your students' cumulative folders will serve as your most basic tool for on-

going evaluation you will need to review them periodically— especially in advance of an evaluation conference. As you and your students reread, compare, and discuss their collected writings, you will easily see evidence of their growth as writers.

In her book, *In the Middle* (Heinemann, 1987), Nancie Atwell suggests that students arrange their writing from the best to the worst in February and again in June. Following these reflective evaluations of their own work, you should arrange a one-to-one conference in which you ask them questions such as the following.

✦ What makes this your best piece?

✦ What are the differences between the best and worst pieces?

✦ What are you able to do as a writer that you couldn't do before?

✦ What problems are you having with your writing?

✦ What do you think you need to work harder at now?

Jot down your students' responses to these questions on a sheet of paper so that you and the student can refer to them periodically. Of course, you can offer your own insights and "nudges" during this conference. If a student says, for example, that his or her best piece is "most interesting," you can ask for an example of an interesting part and an explanation of what made it interesting— such as dialogue, vivid images, and/or description. You also could point out additional strengths and problems that the student failed to mention.

Following are a few examples of the kinds of information students themselves could record.

1. **MY PUBLISHED WORKS** includes a list of titles, dates completed, and the mode or genre of the student's work.

2. **HOW MY WRITING IS CHANGING** includes brief, dated narratives written periodically by the student.

3. **WHAT I CAN DO WHEN I EDIT** includes a list of specific writing conventions and mechanics the student has mastered.

4. **MY POWERFUL WORDS** includes examples of strong verbs, specific nouns, and visual descriptions that have appeared in the student's writing.

5. **MY PERSONAL SPELLING DEMONS** includes a list of frequently misspelled words with check marks to indicate mastery.

INTERVIEWS

There are several kinds of one-to-one interviews. For example, some interviews will provide you with information about each child's **background experiences** and **attitudes** concerning writing, reading, spelling or any other subject area. You can also use interviews to help your students **evaluate their writing** products to determine how effective their writing is and to assess their writing processes—the ways in which they go about developing a piece of writing. Because these interviews meaningfully involve your students in the evaluation process, they become valuable learning experiences in their own right.

CONDUCTING INTERVIEWS

For each different kind of interview—prepare a set of questions in advance to make sure that relevant topics are covered. Of course, determining which questions to ask your students is like selecting a dress or a pair of pants. The fit has to be just right. Therefore, you should choose only those questions that best fit your purposes and your students' developmental level. (*You'll find reproducible questions on pages 79-80.*) It's a good idea to write four to six interview questions on a sheet of paper, leaving several blank lines after each question for your notes. Then make as many copies of the form as you'll need. When the forms are ready, you will also need to prepare your students for their interviews. They might, for example, feel more comfortable about being interviewed if you let them know in advance

that you'd like to learn more about them and about any ideas they may have about writing. As a result, you'll be making notes during the interview to help you remember the interesting things they say.

Allow seven to ten minutes for each interview while the rest of your students are reading independently or are engaged in a task that they can manage on their own. During an interview use plenty of wait time to give a student the opportunity to think about the question before responding. Sometimes you may want to probe more deeply into a particular bit of information by repeating a student's comment or by saying, "That's interesting. Tell me more about that."

Conducting 20 to 30 interviews, of course, takes time—as long as two or three weeks if you conduct a few interviews each day—but they are definitely worthwhile. Administering the same interview two or three times during the year will help you and your students see change and growth in attitudes, behaviors, and knowledge. It is likely, however, that some questions will change as you continually refine and adjust the focus of your observations.

GATHERING BACKGROUND INFORMATION

If you haven't yet conducted any interviews, a background interview is a good place to start. Take some time at the beginning of the school year to get to know your students as writers. By interviewing your students about their writing experiences, you will be better able to assess the learning and feelings that they are bringing with them to your classroom. These interviews also will convey to your students your assumption that they already are developing writers and that writing is a necessary, challenging, and often enjoyable human activity. The following questions will help you learn some important things about your students' attitudes, preferences, and their past writing experiences.

Personal Attitudes

✦ Is it hard or easy for you to write? Why?
✦ What do you like best about writing?

✦ What do you like least about writing?

Home Experiences/Preferences

✦ Do you write at home just because you want to write? What kinds of things do you write at those times?

✦ Where is your favorite place to write?

✦ What kinds of paper and writing tools do you like to use?

✦ Do others in your family write? What do they write?

✦ Who is the best writer you know? What makes his or her writing good?

School Experiences

✦ How did you learn to write?

✦ What do you remember about writing in earlier grades?

✦ What did you write in another grade that was your best writing? What made it good?

The Writing Process

✦ How do you get your ideas for writing?

✦ How do you go about developing a piece of writing? What do you do first, then second, and so on?

✦ What do you do when you get stuck and don't know what to write next?

Personal Goals

✦ What would make writing easier for you in this classroom?

✦ What is something you would most like to see happen during writing time this year?

✦ What is something you need to work on in your writing this year?

WRITING EVALUATION INTERVIEWS

During a writing evaluation interview, you and your students will examine and discuss selected writing samples from their cumulative folders. The purposes of a writing evaluation interview are three-fold: (1) to learn how each student perceives change and growth, (2) to learn the criteria the student uses for evaluating writing, and (3) to

discover the student's new goals. You may want to refer to the previous section in this chapter, "Cumulative Writing Folders," for an example of one kind of evaluation interview. As you read the following additional ideas for interview questions, keep in mind that you will need to limit the number of questions you ask your students if you want the interview time to be manageable.

✦ (Ask after a student has sorted his or her writing pieces into two piles—one with good stories and the other with not such good stories.) How did you decide which ones are good? How do you know when they're not so good?

✦ What modes or forms for writing have you used this year? Which do you prefer? Which didn't work out too well? Which new mode will you try next?

✦ Which piece required the most revisions? What are the major changes you made in your drafts? Can you tell me why you changed these parts? What else do you think you might have changed to improve this piece of writing?

✦ What plans do you have for improving the content of your writing?

✦ Which conventions do you need to work on now?

KEEPING INTERVIEW RECORDS

I've found it to be a great help in the evaluation process to keep the interview forms in a separate set of individual folders, or in your students' cumulative writing folders. You also should give your students easy access to their folders so that they can periodically review their own progress.

Since you probably will be adding additional notes, survey forms, and checklists to each student's folder throughout the year, you may want to consider color-coding the paper you use for the various interviews and forms. Color-coding, of course, makes it easier to locate a specific form as a folder fills up. Any way of organizing the forms that makes sense for you and for your students is fine.

SURVEYS

Surveys are easy to administer to your entire class at one time because your students can write their own responses to the questions. Of course, written responses are less informative because students will say much more when they talk than when they write. Nevertheless, there are several strategies—including the following—you can use with surveys to draw out more thoughtful responses.

1. **Break Apart Big Questions.**
   When writing questions for your survey, always break up big questions into smaller parts. For example, instead of writing "What kinds of things do you like to write?" give your students several choices so they can place checks next to their preferences. (*See Figures 11 and 12, which follow on pages 82 and 83, for background surveys on writing for primary and upper elementary grades.*)

2. **Follow-up Conferences.**
   Follow up interesting or provocative responses to a survey question in a one-to-one conference with a student. If a survey response indicated a negative feeling about writing, for example, you might want to discuss this with the student.

3. **Use Fewer Questions.**
   If you want to elicit more thoughtful responses, spread your survey over three days and use only one or two interview questions each day from the list of interview questions on pages 79–80. Give your students a blank sheet of paper to write on and discuss the questions with them in advance so that they have time to think about what they will write. You will probably see fuller responses on these papers than on a survey sheet. (*See Figure 13, on page 84.*)

CHECKLISTS

You probably already are using checklists right now for many different purposes—such as for revising and editing. Of course, the advantages of all checklists are that they are quick and easy instruments to use and that they help children monitor their own learning. Checklists also let your students know ahead of time what they should aim for when they write. However, because checklists limit the focus of evaluation to only those areas listed on the form, you and your students may miss observing another kind of learning that is occurring.

For example, the checklist AM I READY TO EDIT? (*See Figure 23 on page 103.*) does not take into account a student's ability to use dialogue effectively or whether the student takes risks and experiments with writing. For this reason, it's a good idea to use checklists mainly in conjunction with interviews.

GENERATING CRITERIA FOR CHECKLISTS

To make evaluation meaningful for your students, ask them to help you generate ideas for the writing criteria or traits that should be included on a checklist. Of course, they may not be able to evaluate writing in the first few months of school year, but most students should come into your classroom with some ideas about good writing. For example, early in the year, teachers in the Vermont Writing Project place their students in small groups to brainstorm a list of the traits or criteria that they think define good writing. After comparing their lists, the students then develop a personal class list of the most important criteria. This list changes as they learn more about good writing through mini-lessons, conferences, and sharing sessions in their writing workshops.

The following checklist, Figure 14, was developed in a March brainstorming session with third graders, and the traits reflect what they had learned about writing and the behaviors of writers during the first several months in the third grade as well as their previous school years. After I typed their suggestions as a "Writing Report Card," a form already familiar to the children, each student worked with a partner to discuss and evaluate their best piece of writing. They

FIGURE 11

Name_____ Date _____

BACKGROUND INTERVIEW ON WRITING EXPERIENCES AND ATTITUDES(Primary)

1. Place an X on the face that shows how you feel about writing.

2. What kinds of things do you like to write?

____ animal stories   ____ make-believe   ____ notebook/journal

____ about my own life   ____ poems   ____ notes or messages

____ about facts I learned ____ letters   ____ lists

other _____

3. Which people in your family do you ever see writing? _____

_____

4. What kinds of things do they write? _____

_____

5. What do you write at home? _____

6. What kind of writer do you think you are? _____

7. What will help you become an even better writer? _____

_____

FIGURE 12

Name_____ Date _____

BACKGROUND INTERVIEW ON WRITING EXPERIENCES AND ATTITUDES (Upper Grades)

1. How do you feel when it's time to write? Show it on this scale of 1-5.

1._____ 2._____ 3._____ 4._____ 5._____
   Hate it!   Love it!

2. When you're home, what are all the different kinds of writing you do? (Think of every time you use a pencil and paper)._____

_____

3. What do you most like to write about?_____

4. What steps do you follow when you write a story? What do you do first, second, and so on? _____

_____

5. What do you do to make a piece of writing as good as it can be?

_____

_____

6. What kind of writer do you think you are?_____

7. What do you hope to learn about writing this year? _____

_____

FIGURE 13

Name **Lizzie** Date _____

ATTITUDE TOWARD
WRITING SURVEY

What do you like best about writing?

I like to right, because I can look back and remember thing that i did and i can read it. Sometimes i Laugh at the wrod becase i don't no what they say.

What's hard about writing for you?

It is hard when you don't now what to right

84

checked off the traits with a +, /, or - sign, and then they asked a partner to write comments about their story and their writing behaviors.

DESIGNING A CHECKLIST

As with all evaluation tools, you need to be sure that a checklist you develop focuses on criteria you can realistically expect of most of your students at your particular grade level and in your particular school district. You will also need to consider designing several checklists for different purposes and modes of writing. To evaluate letter writing, for example, you might include aspects of a letter's form—such as heading, greeting, indented body, and closing. You also may want to design a checklist to evaluate the following writing processes. Always keep in mind, however, that shorter checklists make the evaluation process more manageable.

EVALUATING THE ELEMENTS OF GOOD WRITING

The items you use in a checklist for evaluating good writing should relate to whatever you've focused on in your mini-lessons and writing conferences. Also begin such a checklist with writing traits that have to do with the content of a piece of writing. Then place the conventions and mechanics of writing toward the end of the checklist—not because they are unimportant, but because they should be considered only *after* a writer has thoroughly developed a piece of writing.

You can begin to design a checklist of your own by selecting one or two of the most appropriate statements from the categories on page 87. Feel free to abbreviate the statements or even add different ones. *(See Figures 15 and 16 on pages 88 and 89 for examples.)*

WRITING PROCESSES

Name _____   Date _____

_____ ✦ Willing to rethink and revise.

_____ ✦ Experiments and takes risks.

_____ ✦ Offers constructive feedback to others.

_____ ✦ Uses writing time well.

_____ ✦ Understands the difference between revising (e.g., adding and clarifying information) and editing.

_____ ✦ Proofreads for accuracy.

_____ ✦ Uses writing aids in the classroom.(e.g., wall charts, dictionaries, thesauruses)

_____ ✦ Participates during sharing time.

FIGURE 14

Mariko 's Writing Report Card

+ Very Good   ✓ O.K.   − Needs Improvement

QUALITIES OF GOOD WRITING	RATING	COMMENTS By: Elizabeth
FOCUS	✓	I like the way your story is not a big list.
INTERESTING BEGINNINGS	✓	You make It interesting by telling main thing.
COMPLETE MIDDLES: details, dialogue explanations	+	I like how your story is alaways interesting.
ENDINGS that close the story	✓	In my opinion I think you are doing well.
CLEAR WRITING: others understand it	✓	I think you need a little work on that.
CORRECTIONS: punctuation, capitals, spelling, paragraphs	+	I agree you can do that well.
WRITING BEHAVIORS		
USES WRITING TIME WELL	+	I don't no about you but when I get inspired I write write write
CONFERS TO GET IDEAS	✓	I don't blame you for not confering you don't need help.
LISTENS TO AND HELPS OTHERS	✓	You do. you helped me with CATS.

Then use the blank forms (Figures 30 and 31 on pages 110–111 in the Appendix) to structure your own checklist.

Purpose/Meaning

+ The writing shows that the ideas matter to the writer
+ The writer's purpose is clear.
+ The writing has a point or message.

Development/Clarity

+ The writing is developed and understandable.
+ There is sufficient, relevant information.
+ The writer explains, uses examples, and gives reasons.
+ The writing shows visual details.
+ Specific verbs and nouns make pictures or images.
+ Details demonstrate the writer's knowledge of the subject.
+ The writing shows description, explanations, details, and feelings.
+ The writer uses words that appeal to the reader's senses.

Organization

+ The writing shows a focused topic.
+ The narrative has a beginning, middle, and end.
+ The writing has an interesting introduction and ending.
+ The sequence of events is logical.
+ Events are organized in a chronological sequence.
+ Information and ideas are ordered effectively.
+ Narration, description, and dialogue blend together.
+ The title is interesting and relates to the topic

Voice

+ There is a sense of the writer's personal expression and style.
+ The writer's honest point-of-view comes through.
+ The writing is honest and original.

Literary Qualities

+ Story beginnings show effect of literature (A long, long time ago...).
+ The writer creates a mood (humor, suspense, fear).
+ Narratives describe a character's problem and its resolution.

Language

+ The writer uses every day words appropriately.
+ The writer uses specific, precise words.
+ There are few unnecessary words and repetitions.
+ Transitional phrases connect events or ideas (*next, later, meanwhile*).
+ The writing shows sentence variety (declarative sentences, questions, commands, compound sentences, simple sentences).

Conventions and Mechanics

+ The final draft exhibits appropriate mechanics, usage, spelling, and paragraphs.
+ "Chapters" separate different events. (Primary)
+ Paragraphing makes sense.
+ Mechanical errors do not interfere with communication.
+ There are few or no sentence fragments.
+ There are few or no run-on sentences.
+ End punctuation marks are used correctly.
+ Punctuation conventions are used most of the time.
+ Spellings are correct most of the time.
+ Capitals are correctly used most of the time.

Name _____ Grade ____ Date _____

HOW GOOD IS MY WRITING?

~~~~~~

Title of Piece _____

Meaning of Numerical Scores: 4 Shows strength
                              3 Evident
                              2 Beginning to develop
                              1 Not evident yet

The writing shows	Evaluation Score
a focused topic	
a beginning, middle, and ending	
description, details, and feelings	
an interesting title that relates to the topic	
"chapters" that separate different events	
simple and compound sentences	
transitional phrases to connect events (The next . . .)	
end punctuation marks are correct	
capital letters for "I" and first letter of sentences and names	
spellings are correct most of the time (85 – 90%)	

Comments: _____

FIGURE 16

Writer _____ Grade _____ Date _____

HOW GOOD IS MY WRITING?

Title _____

YES	NO		CONTENT QUALITIES
_____	_____	_____	focused on one idea or event _____
_____	_____	_____	supportive details and information _____
_____	_____	_____	organized with interesting lead and ending _____
_____	_____	_____	logical sequence of ideas/events _____
_____	_____	_____	specific, precise words _____
_____	_____	_____	few unnecessary words or repetitions _____
_____	_____	_____	_____
_____	_____	_____	_____

MECHANICS AND CONVENTIONS

_____	_____	_____	paragraph sense _____
_____	_____	_____	few or no punctuation errors _____
_____	_____	_____	few or no capitalization errors _____
_____	_____	_____	few or no spelling errors _____
_____	_____	_____	_____
_____	_____	_____	_____
_____	_____	_____	_____

ANECDOTAL RECORDS

An *anecdotal record* is a brief account of a situation or incident involving one or more students that you have observed. These dated, informal notes usually describe anything that seems important about a student's learning, attitudes, or even social behaviors. The following anecdotal notes, for example, focus on the problems and progress of a single fourth grade student over a period of several days.

Juno S.

2/5 Needs to elaborate story. Had difficult time accepting suggestions in writing conference.

2/7 Came up with a new idea for story but involved killing. No blood or gore in fiction pieces — rule.

2/15 Good ending — space ship.

Although these notes may appear sketchy and unclear to you, they would bring back a vivid picture of the incidents and the writing itself to the teacher who wrote them—even at a later time. Such documented information collected over time will provide evidence of your students' growth and development.

FINDING RECORDING OPPORTUNITIES

You're probably wondering how you will find enough time to keep anecdotal records. The easiest way, of course, is to make it a part of your one-to-one writing conferences. As the following example shows, keep your notes as brief as possible and focus on strengths as well as needs.

James D.

12/4 Humorous dialogue in fishing story. Needs more descrip. and action. Talked more about sister getting sick. Will add. Also needs ¶s and quotes. Excited about writing!

Some teachers also write anecdotal notes when their students are writing in their notebooks. You will find additional opportunities for writing notes as your students learn to conduct their own writing conferences or engage in collaborative projects. The following management ideas may help you make the best use of whatever time you do have.

✦ Use a spiral notebook or three-ring binder with several pages allocated for each student. Use tabs or dividers for their names.

✦ Use five-by-eight index cards alphabetized by your students' names and keep them in a file box.

✦ Use a clipboard with sheets of removable blank address labels. Write the date and student's name on each as you record notes. At the end of the day, peel off the labels and place them on the page or card reserved for each one.

✦ Use a small, softcover notebook or log for reflective writings about your students.

STUDENTS' SHOWCASE PORTFOLIOS

Because students select their own writing samples for portfolios, they are continually engaged in a process of meaningful, reflective evaluation. As they complete new pieces of work, they must use their critical thinking skills when they ask themselves if the new piece is better than another piece in their portfolio. To make that decision, of course, they will have to understand what makes writing good.

Portfolios can also display a student's best work in several subject areas. Based on my own experience, a combined reading-writing portfolio works well because the language arts are naturally interrelated. Much of what I learned about keeping literacy portfolios in my own classroom grew out of a workshop given by Mark Milliken, a fifth grade teacher in Stratham, New Hampshire. His and other helpful articles appear in *Portfolio Portraits* (Heinemann, 1992), edited by Donald Graves and Bonnie Sunstein.

GETTING STARTED

Explain to your students that their portfolios should include the following items:

✦ A range of work samples that show various kinds of work they can do.

✦ Examples of change and improvement—such as in a room or house before and after they worked on it.

✦ Written comments indicating how other people liked their work.

Afterwards, you may want to ask your students to brainstorm ideas of what might go into their own writing portfolios. A fourth grade class generated the following suggestions:

Writing

✦ stories about our lives

✦ fiction

✦ a book review

✦ something written at home

✦ pieces of writing before and after editing to show editing skills

✦ copies of selected entries from writing notebooks

✦ subject area reports

✦ a letter

✦ a newsletter article

✦ poetry

Records for Self-Evaluation

✦ a bar graph of writing modes and genres (*See Figure 17, which follows on page 92.*)

✦ a graph of spelling scores

✦ a list of story titles

✦ comments by readers on a Response Form (*See Figure 29 on page 109.*)

✦ a WHAT I CAN DO WHEN I EDIT list (see pg. 78)

✦ a MY POWERFUL WORDS list (see pg. 79)

✦ a checklist that shows what's good about our writing

✦ the survey on what the class thinks about writing

Let your students have a voice in deciding which of these various types of writing and records should be included in their portfolios. Point out which samples and records you want them to include and then tell them to choose additional ones from the class's brainstormed list. Be sure to tell them that they will use their portfolios to show you and their parents what they are learning about writing. Therefore, they will need to bring in or construct containers for displaying their best work.

HOUSING THE PORTFOLIOS

You will need to discuss with your students the types of containers that they can use to display the contents of their portfolios. You will also need to find a place in your classroom to store the portfolios so that your students can have access to them. If space is limited, use sturdy cartons or rectangular plastic laundry baskets for storing any of the following portfolio containers.

✦ looseleaf three-ring binders

✦ "trapper–keeper" type notebooks with pocketed folders

✦ photo albums

✦ a box of clear plastic page protectors

✦ an attache case (second hand) with a three-ring binder

✦ an expandable manila envelope

ORGANIZING PORTFOLIO CONTENTS

If you want your students to share their portfolios with their parents at the same time they bring home their report cards, they should begin organizing the contents two or three weeks before. By starting early, they will also have time to discuss the samples and records in a conference with you.

Once your students understand the purpose of a portfolio, they will need your help in selecting and organizing its contents. To help them do this, make the following suggestions about the contents that appear on page 93 under "Helping Students Reflect".

FIGURE 17

Name_____ School Year _____

WRITING GENRE CHART

Number of Completed Pieces

	1	2	3	4	5	6	7	8	9	10
personal experience										
memoir										
informational article or report										
letter										
poem/song										
fantasy										
realistic fiction										
myth/legend folktale										
play										
news story										
"how-to"										
brochure or guidebook										

Yellow	Red	Blue
Sept. – Nov.	Dec. – March	April – June

A Checklist

Have your students make a checklist that includes all the samples and records—your choices and their own—that they plan to include in their portfolio. As they collect each sample for the portfolio, they should check it off.

Before and After Samples

To show how well they can use the conventions and mechanics of writing *independently*, your students should revise and recopy one unedited piece of writing completed at a previous time. To avoid making this task too burdensome or time consuming, have them select a short piece of writing such as a letter or a notebook entry. Remind your students to date the before and after samples.

Samples of Best Work

Although your students may have selected a "best piece," at an earlier date, ask them to review the work in their cumulative writing folders to see if they have written an even better piece. (*See The "Post-It" Contest on this page and page 94.*)

Records and Charts

If your students have been keeping records—such as lists of titles, genre charts, and spelling progress graphs—they will probably have to bring them up to date.

A Sample from Home

Discuss with your students the various possibilities of writing that they do on their own—such as letters, notes, shopping lists, and cartoon stories. If some say they've written a letter but can't bring it in because it was mailed, tell them to include the letter they received in response or to write about the letter—for example, who they wrote to and why. Others may want to bring in a special piece of writing completed in an earlier grade.

Cover Letters

Have your students write about their growth as writers and include their observations as a part of their portfolios. You will find that these written insights will become powerful aids for communicating with parents. Your students can write a single lengthy piece of writing that covers every portfolio sample, or they can write separate short letters for each sample. Shorter letters, of course, work best for second, third, and fourth graders. Encourage your students to develop their cover letters just as they would any writing piece—by drafting, conferring, revising, and recopying.

A Table of Contents

After all the samples and their cover letters have been collected, have your students number the pages. After they write a table of contents, provide a three-hole punch so that they can place their pages in three-ring binders.

HELPING STUDENTS REFLECT

Let your students know in advance of a conference that you will ask them to tell you what each portfolio selection—writing pieces as well as record forms—shows that they can do as a writer. Of course, reflective analysis will be difficult for them at first, but by the time they are working on their portfolios, they will probably have completed several pieces of work and developed a pretty good understanding of the criteria you use to evaluate writing. You can also use the following strategies to encourage your students to reflect on their growth and strengths as writers.

Group Evaluation Conferences

Meet with several students at one time. Then after a student shares a piece of writing or a record form, ask everyone in the group to comment on the strengths of the selection.

The "Post-It" Contest

After your students have reviewed the traits they have been using to evaluate writing, ask them to reread their writing pieces to select one or two of their best works. Tell them to place a "Post-It" note over each good part and explain what makes that part so good. The piece with the most sticky papers should be considered the "winner." Then ask your students to refer to their notes as they write you a letter that tells why that piece is their best. (This letter should be placed in the portfolio along with the writing selection.) Following is a sample letter that a fourth grader wrote about a story she had written in three chapters.

> *"I think this writing is good because it is beliveble, realistic, and funny. One of the funny things is: Mrs. Muldoon asked Mr. Muldoon, "I guess we should give these guys a tip?" Lauren answer "Are you kidding?!"*
>
> *I made the story beleveable by making it have problems, such as in Pajama Mix-Ups [Chapter 3] I lost my pajamas and I couldn't find them and Lauren lost her ski on the chairlift [Chapter 1], the story was also beliveable because everything realy happend."*

Guiding Questions

Give your students a guide—such as the following—to use when evaluating their record forms and writing notebooks. Working together with a classmate also helps younger students develop and articulate their insights. However, you may want to have upper elementary students put their ideas in writing.

WHAT TO LOOK FOR IN YOUR WRITING RECORDS

1. What does your mode and genre graph show about you as a writer? (*See Figure 17 on page 92.*) Look at the yellow rectangles on the bar graph that represent the kinds of writing you did from September to November. What kinds of writing did you usually choose to do then? Look at the red rectangles that represent the writing you did from December through March. What changes do you see? What kinds of writing do you think you will try next?

2. What do the lists on your cumulative writing folder show about you as a writer? Think about how many pieces you've published, how long you usually worked on a piece, what editing skills you used, and what powerful language you included.

3. What does your writing notebook show about you as a writer? How many entries have you written? What have you learned about your writing as you reread your entries? What different kinds of writing have you tried? Which notebook entries were later developed and published?

4. Look at the "Background Survey on Writing" form that you filled out earlier in the year. (*See Figure 11 or 12 on page 82 or 83.*) Which of the feelings and experiences you described then have changed? Which are the same? What information could you add now?

HOLDING PORTFOLIO CONFERENCES

In advance of a conference, look through a student's portfolio and note some areas or concerns that you want to discuss with that student. It's a good idea to hold your conferences as soon as your students have organized their portfolios. You should be able to manage one-to-one conferences easily because your students will be completing their portfolios at different times since some will still be updating their various record forms and writing about their portfolios' contents as others are finishing. Of course, you will need to suggest independent activities for students who complete their portfolio conferences so that you can meet individually with the rest of the class.

One way to begin conferences is to ask your students what each record or sample shows about them as writers. Because students don't always notice all that a sample shows about what they know, you may need to point out additional strengths as well as some areas they need to work on. After discussing a portfolio sample or record, ask your students about new goals and plans they have, based on what they have learned during the conference. The brief notes you should take during conferences will provide insightful information for parent conferences as well as reminders of areas you will want to follow up on in future conferences with your students.

The following notes are excerpted from a

PORTFOLIO CONFERENCE NOTES		
Record Sample	**Student's Comments**	**Goals**
Revised letter	I know how to spell "Sincerely." I learned to write the abbrev. for month. I learned to line up "Sincerely" with date. I made it make sense by adding more details. I can make 2 short sentences into one.	Indent body, put comma after Sincerely

full page of portfolio conference notes I made during a conference with a fourth grade student. This excerpt focuses on a revised, self-edited letter. After comparing the revised letter with his first draft, my student explained what the final letter showed he had learned to do as a writer. After he stated his goals for further improving his letter writing skills, I suggested an additional one. My notes of the student's oral responses appear somewhat abbreviated and disjointed because I tried to write just enough to capture his meaning.

CONSIDERING PROBLEMS AND REWARDS OF PORTFOLIOS

There's no denying that showcase portfolios require effort and time because you are asking your students to record information, review their work with criteria in mind, and write about their progress. Self-evaluation not only places a good deal of responsibility on youngsters, but it also places a good deal of responsibility on you to guide them through mini-lessons and conferences so that they can arrive at new understandings and strategies for improving their writing.

My personal experiences with student portfolios, however, show me that the time spent is definitely worthwhile. I believe that individual portfolios make students feel competent; in fact, I've never had a student who did not progress from one point to a higher one. Everyone can do something well, and portfolios show this. On the other hand, everyone has something that needs work, and portfolio conferences reveal this, too. I've

also discovered that when students are part of a realistic and individualized evaluation process, they are more likely to achieve their goals.

Parent education and involvement are additional benefits of showcase portfolios. Following an Open School Night when I showed parents examples of what they might expect to see in their children's portfolios, several parents commented on how the presentation gave them a clear idea of what their children would be learning during the year. Although I hadn't realized it, the portfolios visually communicated to the parents my language arts curriculum as well as my students' learning goals.

The parents even become part of the evaluation process when I send the portfolios home with each report card. In the following letter, I invite parents to confer with their children by asking the same questions that I ask them in their portfolio conferences. Then I ask the parents to write their reactions on the bottom of the letter and return it to me.

Parents usually respond positively and knowledgeably to such a portfolio experience. The following responses particularly delighted me because the students had previously experienced some problems with reading or writing.

"Jimmy and I have examined his portfolio. I am very happy to see the progress he has made in writing as well as reading. His confidence in himself has increased a great deal and he now is not afraid to read a book that looks too hard or write a story even if he is unable to master the spelling."

"...Ron's writing is now done in script and is gradually improving in accuracy and fluency. The content of his writing is more developed and well thought out. He has outlined a clear plan to further improve the content of his writing. I am very proud of his progress and have told him this."

THE VALUE OF EVALUATION AND ASSESSMENT

I have discovered that by including my students and their parents in the evaluation process, I have real partners in the business of teaching and learning. What's more, each of us gains something of value. My students have more control over their own development and no longer depend on me to wield the carrot and stick for them to try harder, and their parents know a great deal more about our curriculum and goals. Best of all, I have a better understanding of my students as learners and as people, and this affects the way I teach.

If you are wondering whether a shared evaluation process will work for you and your students, give yourself time to experiment with the changes this chapter suggests. The important thing is to trust yourself as you try out new approaches. Don't take too big a bite at first; select only a few strategies and adapt them to fit your needs. Consider any setbacks as learning-in-progress, read as much as you can, attend workshops, and keep an open mind as you engage in the evolving process of evaluation and assessment.

Dear Parents,

As March comes to a close, it is time to let you know once again how your child is doing in language arts. That's why I'm sending you an updated portfolio with current samples of your child's best work in writing and reading. As you already know, the selections were made by your child and were discussed in a conference with me.

Please take ten minutes or so to look over the portfolio as your child explains what each sample shows. Following are some questions you might ask this time.

✦ What does this tell me about you as a writer (or reader)?

✦ How has your work changed since the end of November?

✦ What do you think you need to work harder at now?

I think you will enjoy looking at the contents of the portfolio and hearing what your child has to say. Afterwards, however, I will appreciate your sharing your reactions with me by filling out the tear-off form below. We will use the portfolios in the classroom until the end of the year.

Sincerely,

I reviewed my child's portfolio. Here are my reactions.

_____

_____

_____

Questions Teachers Ask About Assessing and Evaluating Writing

Q What do you say when a parent asks, "How does my child's work compare with the work of the other students in the class?"

A This question seldom comes up once parents are given a good picture of their child's growth, strengths, and goals through portfolios and other assessment records. On the few occasions that it has, I have usually referred to specific examples of the child's work and have said, "This shows that Tim can.... About half of my students can do this, too, or, one area that Tim seems to be having more trouble with than most other students is ....."

Q What do you say to parents who focus on the mistakes in spelling, punctuation, and other conventions when they look at their children's writing?

A I address this important issue when parents come to Open School Night or to a lunchtime PTA meeting. I read aloud a well-written story by a student and ask the parents to tell me what the writer did to make the writing good. Then after I show them what the draft looked like before it was edited, I explain the editing process. I also let them know that journal or notebook writings are valued for thoughtful ideas and are not corrected.

Q We have to give our students grades on report cards. How do you translate the evaluation process you described into letters and/or numbers?

A This isn't difficult to do if the traits and processes you evaluate in your classroom correspond to the traits and processes listed on the report card. For this reason, teachers in the schools in my district work together to revise home report forms every few years. The best way I've found to communicate progress on the report form, however, is through written comments that are based on my records and on the students' portfolios.

Q Are there any school-wide systems for extending student writing portfolios throughout the grades?

A Students in Vermont schools keep writing portfolios, containing three or four pieces of writing from each school year, throughout high school. Using an analytic assessment guide, teachers evaluate writing in fourth and eighth grades. In these grades, students collect specific writing samples—such as a "best piece" and a letter about the best piece; a piece of writing from any curriculum area that is not defined as "English;" a poem, story, play, or personal narrative; a response to a cultural event, public exhibit, sports event, book, current issue, or a math or science phenomenon.

FIGURE 18

HOW TO FIND A TOPIC

1. Reread your writing notebook.

2. Look through your ALL ABOUT ME folder.

3. Read some books in our picture book collection to find a personal memory that a story brings to your mind.

4. Think of a time when you felt happy, sad, scared, angry, or proud. Visualize the experience with your eyes closed—look, listen, and think.

5. Check or write three things on an IDEAS FOR STORYTELLING form. Ask a friend to interview you about each topic.

FIGURE 19

WHAT WRITERS DO

1. Look for three things you could write about that you remember fairly well. Write them down.

2. Break up a big topic into smaller parts.

3. Tell someone your stories and write down things you want to remember.

4. Pick the topic that means the most to you. Write a temporary title and a draft.

5. Talk more about your story in a conference.

6. Revise and change parts, if necessary.

7. Write an interesting introduction.

8. Work on a satisfying ending. Have a conference.

9. Try out different titles.

10. Fill out an AM I READY TO EDIT? form. Have a conference.

11. Fill out an EDITING STEPS form.

12. Give the edited draft to your teacher.

13. Illustrate a cover. Print the title and author's name.

FIGURE 20

WHAT TO DO WHEN YOU ARE STUCK

✦ Write in your writing notebook.

✦ Make a Storyboard:

    1. Fold a paper into six boxes.

    2. Number the boxes from 1 through 6.

    3. Draw the six most important events in the boxes.

    4. Draw stick figures to represent the characters.

    5. Use "speech bubbles" to show dialogue.

1.	2.	3.
4.	5.	6.

✦ Write about the new parts you drew.

✦ Write 3 different titles for your story.

✦ Write a dedication page.

✦ Write an "about the author" page.

FIGURE 21

HOW TO HELP A WRITER

Ask: "What would you like help with?"

Listen

Say: "Tell us what you're writing about."

Listen

Respond to the writer's stated need.

Ask about something you don't understand or want to know more about.

Listen

Say: "Here's what you told me." (Repeat the writer's words.)

Suggest some things the writer might want to try.

Ask: "What will you do next?"

FIGURE 22

MARKS FOR REVISING AND EDITING

MARK	WHAT IT DOES	EXAMPLE
ℓ	Deletes (takes out) letters, words, sentences, lines, punctuation marks	I went ice skating. ~~I went~~ on Friday.
∧	Adds (inserts) letters, words, sentences	When I was ~~little~~, I had a stuffed animal. *(five inserted; f and dog and e inserted)*
≡	Changes a lower case letter to a capital letter	i visited my grandparents on thanksgiving.
/	Changes a capital letter to a lower case letter	The Zoo was fun. I saw Zebras and Lions.
⌣	Combines two words or parts of words	I saw some thing move in the bushes.
#	Makes a space between two words.	I like vanilla ice cream.

FIGURE 23

Name_____ Date _____

AM I READY TO EDIT?

Name of Editing Partner _____

Title _____

1. I read the writing to myself to see if it made sense.   _____

2. I read it to my editing partner to see if it made sense.   _____

3. My writing is focused on one important idea or topic.   _____

4. I developed the topic with enough information.   _____

5. Visual details show the reader what is happening.   _____

6. My introduction attracts a reader's attention.   _____

7. The title fits the story and gets a reader interested.   _____

8. The ending ties up the story.   _____

9. My teacher heard or read my writing.   _____

10. Writing this piece was hard work _____ not so hard _____ easy _____.

Comments: _____

_____

FIGURE 24

Name_____ Date _____

EDITING STEPS (Primary)

Title _____

Editing Partner_____

I read my story to a friend to see if it made sense. _____

I read my story to a friend to see where to **STOP** for

periods .   question marks ?   exclamation points !

I deleted extra words (and, then) that I didn't need. _____

I used capital letters at the beginning of each sentence _____

        for the first letter of a name _____

        for the word "I" _____

I underlined words that may be misspelled.

        Example: We <u>plad</u> a game. _____

I gave my edited draft to my teacher. _____

FIGURE 25

Name_____ Date _____

EDITING STEPS (Upper Grades)

Title _____

1. I replaced weak words with specific words. (went, nice)   _____

2. I deleted unnecessary words by combining short sentences.   _____

3. I deleted over-used words. (then, and, so)   _____

4. I checked for correct punctuation. (. ? ! , " " ')   _____

5. I checked for correct capitalization.   _____

6. I indented or used a paragraph symbol (¶) to begin

   a new paragraph.   _____

7. I underlined words that I think may be incorrectly spelled.   _____

8. I gave my edited draft to my editing partner to check.   _____

9. I gave my edited draft to my teacher to check.   _____

10. I completed a TRY AGAIN! spelling form.   _____

I think my editing skills are

   1. Yucky _____   2. Improving_____   3. Pretty good_____

FIGURE 26

POSSIBLE WAYS TO PUBLISH

essay

poem

letter

picture storybook

"Big Book"

play script

magazine article

travel brochure

how-to-do-it book

guidebook or handbook

song

fact book

riddle book

newsletter

cartoon story

scroll story

review of a book, movie, or event

FIGURE 27

SURVEY OF
DAILY WRITING PLANS

NAMES OF STUDENTS	DATE _____	DATE _____	DATE _____

FIGURE 28

NOTEBOOK ENTRY OF A FICTIONAL CHARACTER

Ten-year-old Anastasia Krupnik was angry. Her teacher, Mrs. Westvessel, had given her an F on her poem because it didn't rhyme. In the following excerpt we see how Anastasia uses her writing notebook to express her feelings.

"… [Anastasia] turned the pages of her notebook until she came to a blank one, page fourteen, and printed carefully at the top of the right-hand side THINGS I HATE.

She thought very hard because she wanted it to be an honest list.

Finally she wrote down: "Mr. Belden at the drugstore." Anastasia honestly hated Mr. Belden, because he called her "girlie," and because once, in front of a whole group of fifth grade boys who were buying baseball cards, he had said the rottenest, rudest, thing she could ever imagine anyone saying..."You want some Cover-up Kreme for those freckles, girlie?"

Next, without any hesitation, Anastasia wrote down "Boys." She honestly hated boys. All of the fifth grade boys buying baseball cards that day had laughed.

"Liver" was also an honest thing. Everybody in the world hated liver except her parents.

And she wrote down "pumpkin pie," after some thought. She had tried to like pumpkin pie, but she honestly hated it.

And finally, Anastasia wrote, at the end of her THINGS I HATE list: "Mrs. Westvessel." That was the most honest thing of all.

Then, to even off the page, she made a list on the left-hand side: THINGS I LOVE. For some reason it was an easier list to make.

From *Anastasia Krupnik*
by Lois Lowry
NY: Houghton Mifflin, 1979.

FIGURE 29

Name _____ Date _____

RESPONSE FORMS
FOR READERS

〜〜〜〜〜〜〜〜〜〜〜〜〜〜〜〜〜〜〜〜〜〜〜〜〜〜〜〜〜〜〜

Please tell the author something you liked about the story!

Title _____

Author _____

Readers' names	Comments
_____	_____
_____	_____
_____	_____
_____	_____
_____	_____
_____	_____
_____	_____
_____	_____
_____	_____

FIGURE 30

Name _____ Grade _____ Date _____

HOW GOOD IS MY WRITING?

Title of Piece _____

Meaning of Numerical Scores: 4 Shows strength
                                      3 Evident
                                      2 Beginning to develop
                                      1 Not evident yet

The writing shows:	Evaluation Score

Comments: _____

FIGURE 31

Writer _____ Grade _____ Date _____

WRITING EVALUATION SCALE

Title _____

YES		NO	CONTENT QUALITIES
_____	_____	_____	focused on one idea or event _____
_____	_____	_____	supportive details and information _____
_____	_____	_____	organized with interesting lead and ending ____
_____	_____	_____	logical sequence of ideas / events _____
_____	_____	_____	specific, precise words _____
_____	_____	_____	few unnecessary words or repetitions _____
_____	_____	_____	_____
_____	_____	_____	_____

MECHANICS AND CONVENTIONS

_____	_____	_____	paragraph sense _____
_____	_____	_____	few or no punctuation errors _____
_____	_____	_____	few or no capitalization errors _____
_____	_____	_____	few or no spelling errors _____
_____	_____	_____	few or no run-on sentences _____
_____	_____	_____	_____
_____	_____	_____	_____

References

Calkins, Lucy M.
The Art of Teaching Writing.
NH: Heinemann, 1986.

Calkins, Lucy M. with Shelley Harwayne
Living Between the Lines.
NH: Heinemann, 1991.

Graves, Donald H.
Writing: Teachers & Children at Work.
NH: Heinemann, 1993.

Graves, Donald H. and Bonnie S. Sunstein (eds.).
Portfolio Portraits.
NH: Heinemann, 1992.

Kovacs, Deborah and James Preller
Meet the Authors and Illustrators.
NY: Scholastic, 1991.

Lloyd, Pamela
How Writers Write.
NH: Heinemann, 1989.

Trelease, Jim
The Read Aloud Handbook.
NY: Penguin, 1985.